Only a child –
Yet I am nearer to creation
My colours new and vivid
Chaotic and joyful
Give me the means and let me be free
To make sense of the world
As it unfolds around me
I will learn from you
But you can learn from me, if you
Cherish the life that I bring
And listen.

Di Brewster, 1996

<u>Acknowledgements</u>

I would like to acknowledge the huge contribution that Georgia and her parents, Ian and Colette, have made to this book. I have learnt a great deal from them during our discussions about Georgia. They have been very committed to gathering the diary record and to reflecting on and analysing what happened. They have both given me critical feedback on my representation of our discussions.

I would also like to thank Eloise for her meticulous proof reading of the manuscript, helpful critical feedback and for her witty comments.

I want to thank Tina Bruce as an editor and friend for encouraging me to write this book and for her frequent feedback on every aspect of the work. All of my colleagues at Pen Green have been supportive and interested, but a special mention must go to Margy Whalley for constantly inspiring me and for believing in my ability to write well.

Last, but not least, I want to thank Terry for shopping, cooking and sorting out the computer, and Paul for our Sunday afternoon chats about the wider world.

Cath Arnold

CONTENTS

SERIES PREFACE – 0–8 YEARS

At most times in history and in most parts of the world, the first eight years of life have been seen as the first phase of living. Ideally, during this period, children learn who they are; about those who are significant to them; and how their world is. They learn to take part, and how to contribute creatively, imaginatively, sensitively and reflectively.

Children learn through and with the people they love, and the people who care for them. They learn through being physically active, through real, direct experiences, and through learning how to use and make symbolic systems, such as play, language and representation.

Whether children are at home, in nursery schools, classes, family centres, day nurseries, playgroups (now re-named preschools), workplace nurseries or primary schools, they need informed adults who can help them.

The 0–8 series will help those who work with young children, in whatever capacity, to be as informed as possible about this first phase of living.

From the age of 8 years old, the developing and learning can be consolidated, hopefully in ways which build on what has gone before.

In this series, each book emphasises a different aspect of the first stage of living (0–8 years).

Getting To Know You: A Guide to Record Keeping in Early Childhood Education and Care by Lynne Bartholomew and Tina Bruce is based on principles of good practice in the spirit of Stephen Isaacs. It explores the relationship between observation, assessment, evaluation and monitoring in a record keeping system. It takes account of legal requirements in the different parts of the UK. The book is full of examples of good practice in record keeping. Unless we know and understand our children, unless we act effectively on what we know, we cannot help them very much.

Learning to be Strong: Integrating Education and Care in Early Childhood by Margy Whalley is an inspirational book. Pen Green Centre for Under-fives and their Families in Corby, Northamptonshire, is an acknowledged beacon of excellence, emulated throughout the UK and internationally. When adults come together as a team – parents, educators, carers, those in Social Services and Health experts using their energy on behalf of the child – then education and care become truly integrated. Just as it was important that Margaret McMillan's pioneer work at the turn of the century in integrating education and care should be recorded, so this book has become a classic of the 1990s.

Beacons of excellence, like Pen Green, when documented in this way, can continue to illuminate principles which influence quality practice through the ages, transcending the passing of time.

Helping Children to Draw and Paint in Early Childhood: Children and Visual Representation by John Matthews gives a fascinating insight into the early drawings, paintings and models that children make. The book shows how these begin and traces development from scribbles to later drawings in the period of the first eight years. A wealth of real life examples is given, together with practical stategies that adults can use to help children develop their drawings and paintings with quality.

In *Helping Children to Learn through a Movement Perspective*, Mollie Davies, an internationally respected movement expert with years of practical experience of working with young children, writes about the central places of movement within the learning process. In a lively, well-illustrated book, with lots of real examples, she makes a case for movement as a common denominator of the total development of children, and in this draws our attention to its integrating function. A whole chapter is devoted to dance – the art form of movement. The provision of a readily accessible movement framework gives excellent opportunities for adults to plan, observe and record their children's development in movement terms.

Self-Esteem and Successful Early Learning by Rosemary Roberts is about the importance of being positive, encouraging and gently firm in bringing up and working with young children. Whilst every family is different, every family shares some aspects of living with young children. These are taken up and given focus in the book in ways that are accessible and lead to practical strategies. The reader meets a variety of situations with the family and explores successful ways of tackling them so that the theories supporting the practice become meaningful and useful.

The Development of Language and Literacy by Marion Whitehead emphasises the importance of adults being sensitive to the child's culture, feeling and ideas as language develops and early attempts to communicate in writing and reading emerge. Bilingualism and its indications are looked at in depth. Children need to spend time with people who care about them, enjoy being with them, and sensitively support their early language and literacy.

Resources for Early Learning: Children, Adults and Stuff by Pat Gura takes a critical look at the materials that are given to children in early years settings and examines the conventional wisdom and assumptions that early years workers make about resources such as sand, water, paint, blocks, the home area and others. The book encourages practitioners to be reflective.

Effective Early Learning edited by Christine Pascal and Tony Bertram is about practitioner research. It shows how nine very different early childhood settings experienced the Effective Early Learning project. This research project is about empowering practitioners to develop their own practice and is having a great influence and impact on the quality of practice in the UK.

Clinging to dogma, 'I believe children need. . .' or saying 'What was good enough for me . . .' is not good enough. Children deserve better than that. The pursuit of excellence means being informed. This series will help adults to increase their knowledge and understanding of the 'first phase of living', and to act in the light of this for the good of children.

TINA BRUCE

Introducing Georgia

This book is the story of Georgia. It is about her development and learning between the ages of 2 and 5 years. Of course, no two children develop and learn in exactly the same way, but it is still helpful to follow one child in depth. Looking at Georgia's unique ways of learning, can lead us to discover the similarities between her and other children growing up in the UK today. As Bruce (et al, 1995) comment,

> By exploring differentiation, or differences between children, there is the possibility of making progress in teasing out the essentials, the universals.

There are many things to consider. These include Georgia's gender, her position in the family, and her likes and dislikes. Each of these features provides learning opportunities for Georgia – this is true of every child in every family. When Georgia starts nursery at 3 years of age, she brings with her a wealth of experience. The nursery workers can use these experiences as a base on which to build and to plan further learning experiences.

In order to tell Georgia's story, this book uses narrative observations, gathered over time by her parents at home (parent diary) and by workers at nursery. Narrative observations are useful because they:

- help us to analyse in many different ways

- encourage discussion, in retrospect, about Georgia's learning; discussions take place between her parents, a worker (who is the author) and Georgia herself

- help us to plan for Georgia's future learning.

In order to help us get to know Georgia, in Chapter One we will meet Georgia and her family. We will learn about Georgia's home context in some detail and about her transition to nursery.

Before we can begin to look at Georgia's development and learning, we need to make sure we are equipped to make sense of what we see. Theories help us to do this. For this reason, Chapter Two begins by outlining the theories and traditions in early childhood education and care. We will draw on these as we observe Georgia's development and learning. This chapter also explores two possible ways of analysing observations of Georgia and suggests the types of staff training necessary to help us to learn about children's development and learning.

Chapter Three is a record of Georgia learning to write and read, acknowledging her early mark-making, stories, rhymes and role play as part of that process.

Chapter Four traces Georgia's understanding of some mathematical concepts, such as number, quantity, division, size, fit, time and chronology.

Chapter Five charts Georgia's developing scientific concepts including food allergy, childbirth and changes in state.

Chapter Six examines Georgia's emotional development by looking at issues of power, change and uncertainty in her life and at how adults help her to cope with and to learn from periods of change.

Chapter Seven concludes the book by describing how adults help Georgia to make connections across the curriculum during her year at nursery. We also build a picture of Georgia as she starts school and we consider her interests at 7 years of age.

IMPORTANT EVENTS IN GEORGIA'S LIFE

Georgia's age	Event
2 years 3 months	Harry (Georgia's brother) is born
2 years 7 months	Georgia starts playgroup
2 years 10 months	Harry has his first allergic reaction
2 years 10 months	Dad changes job – works for Kai
3 years 5 months	Dad changes job – works for Jane
3 years 7 months	Georgia starts nursery
3 years 8 months	Mum starts working evenings
3 years 11 months	Dad is made redundant and is out of work for 2 months
3 years 11 months	Mum begins working mornings and extra hours
4 years 1 month	Dad begins training then working evenings
4 years 7 months	Georgia starts school
5 years	Parents decide to separate
5 years 1 month	Mum begins full-time work
Over next 5 months	Parents negotiate and establish pattern of care, which is only possible because dad's working hours are flexible.
5 years 6 months	Mum buys house and moves out – children sleep at mum's from Monday to Friday and at dad's Saturday and Sunday. Dad collects children from mum's each weekday morning and takes them to school or carer. At the end of the day, dad collects children from school or carer and either he brings them to her at work or she collects them from him at home. Mum continues working days and dad continues working evenings.

1 INTRODUCING GEORGIA AND HER FAMILY

It is when we are dealing with people and things in the context of fairly immediate goals and intentions and familiar patterns of events that we feel most at home. (Donaldson, 1978)

In this chapter we meet Georgia, aged 2 years, and learn about her experiences in her family.

- Georgia's home.

- Who Georgia knows.

- Where Georgia goes.

- Georgia's play, both at home and at nursery.

Before we explore these ideas, we might remember what Margaret Donaldson wrote about the kinds of learning that will make human sense to Georgia at this point. In the 1970s Donaldson extended Jean Piaget's theory. She and her colleagues discovered that, often, problems did not make any 'human sense' to children (Donaldson, 1978). Unless problems make human sense, they are 'isolated from the rest of existence'. Young children, in their quest for knowledge and understanding of the world, are seeking to make connections between experiences. They continuously bring their earlier, familiar experiences to bear on new situations and problems. So, using problems disconnected from a child's previous experiences, is neither fair to the child nor likely to provide information about what a child knows or wants to know. If we are to give each child an equal chance in education, we must actively seek to discover what experiences they already have, in order that we might help them to make connections between new knowledge and their earlier experiences.

This discovery, that children function at a much higher level when what they learn makes human sense to them, along with renewed interest in Vygotsky's ideas about the importance of the social context of learning, sit well together. This is called a **social constructivist** or **interactionist approach**. This approach acknowledges that each child must explore and discover things for him or herself (**Piagetian theory**), while attributing equal importance to the people with whom the child interacts (**Vygotskerian theory**).

GEORGIA'S HOME

When Georgia was born, her dad had lived in the same house for 10 years. For three of those years, her mum shared the house with him. It is a detached house. It has an open plan garden at the front and a back garden which can be accessed either through the garage or through the living room of the house. The back garden is big enough for a sandpit, paddling pool and small slide as well as other toys. Georgia's family garden consists of a small patio and grass. There are 10 houses in the close. They are in a circle facing inwards. The front gardens are not enclosed and several are used by children to play together. When Georgia was born there were already seven children living in the close, all girls. The only cars that come into the close either belong to the families who live there or to people who are visiting those families.

Looking back with Georgia's parents

Looking back on Georgia's early life, Georgia's parents realise something that only now seems significant, happened soon after Georgia was born. Some of the older children in the close began to take an interest in her.

> **Dad:** *'The older girls paid her a lot of attention – they used to ask to come into the house.'*
> **Mum:** *'Amy and Jennifer came and asked to play with Georgia because they liked babies.'*

Amy and Jennifer are non-identical twins, at the time aged 7, who live next door but one.

Georgia's parents took her out into the close from the time that she was four or five months old. That way, she got to know other people and they got to know her.

> **Dad:** *'You just have to take a baby or toddler out and other children come.'*
> **Mum:** *'The older children kept her amused.'*

Georgia seemed to enjoy the company of other people, particularly the children. Soon, two other children, only months younger than her, are born: James (next door) and Little Emma (three houses away). Later, Georgia, James and Little Emma all start school together at 4 years old.

Gradually, Georgia begins to play outside in the close. At first her parents go outside with her. Soon they begin keeping an eye on her from the house. Again the physical layout of the house is important.

> **Dad:** *'Most kitchens look out on the close.'*

Other parents are either out with or watching out for their children who are playing in the close.

The advantages of living in a close

> **Mum:** *'If you live in a street, you can only let your child play in the garden. If other children come into the garden, then I would be responsible for them as well as my own child. The close is a sort of public place. I only have to be responsible for my own child there, although I would look out for the others.'*

In the close the adults can take some joint responsibility for what happens. Georgia's parents consider the close to be 'a safe environment'. It's not just the parents who help to create this atmosphere: the older children are genuinely interested in including a younger child in their play.

How Georgia's home affects her development and learning

The physical layout of the close enables each family to observe what other families are doing when they come out of their houses or when they look out of a window which faces the close. In a small close like this, the various activities of the people seem to take precedence over everything else. The layout of the houses in a circle facing in helps to foster a spirit of a community among the people who live there. Going out into the close enables Georgia, not only to get to know the people, but also to begin to understand the 'social meanings' of the cultural context in which the family live (Blanck, 1990).

Georgia is the firstborn child in her family and, therefore, it is fairly quiet in her house. However, step outside the front door and there is a great deal of stimulation, mostly from the people who live in the close. Georgia gains knowledge early on about the latest trends, for example, friendship bracelets and braids. She knows about the games currently being played, for example 'tig'. At 3 years 7 months she listens carefully to what the older children tell her.

Georgia plays with older children out in the close

Georgia has had two friendship bracelets on for about two weeks now. They're the current trend – Nicola made them for her. When she came in with them on she said,'have to keep them on at bath time, shower time, bed time and all the time. Them allowed wet, them just dry.' Obviously trying to repeat what Nicola had told her.
(Parent Diary)

WHO GEORGIA KNOWS

Attachment

Georgia gets to know her immediate family (mum and dad), extended family – grandparents, aunt and uncle – and the people who live in the close. She is very closely attached to her mum, dad, aunty Eloise and Jennifer. Jennifer is one of the 7-year-old twins, who live next door but one. Attachment to important people 'spells security' for Georgia (Schaffer, 1995).

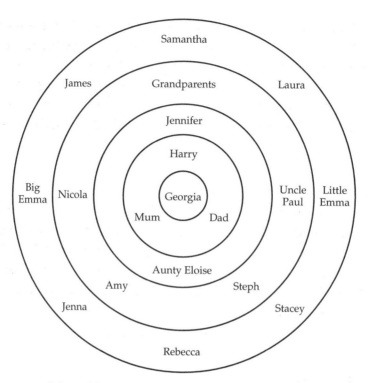

Adapted from Bronfenbrenner's Ecology of Human Development (Henry, 1996)

When Georgia learns to talk, she calls Eloise 'Aya', her maternal uncle Paul 'Pob', Jennifer 'Gaga' and Amy (the other twin) 'Meemy'. She also attempts to say James (3 months her junior and living next door). She calls him 'Mem'. Pinker (1994) speculates that babies and young children communicate words connected to their interests just as adults do. The diagram above shows how closely attached Georgia is to the people in her life. So, Georgia is most closely attached to her parents and brother (when he is born) and merely acquainted with Samantha (who is placed in the outer circle of the diagram).

Harry is born

When her brother, Harry, is born Georgia is 2 years 3 months old. She frequently engages in role play which includes babies and buggies. Georgia likes to be the 'mummy' or the 'baby'. Her role seems to depend on who else is playing. Faulkner (1995) describes George Herbert Mead's theory:

He claimed that the experience of role-play and pretence in early childhood was vital for the development of the self.

As well as getting to know those people with whom she has frequent, direct contact, Georgia is interested in and has knowledge of people her parents speak about but whom she sees rarely. When she was born her dad had worked at the same toy firm for over 10 years. He took her to the office when she was a baby. Georgia's dad's boss of 10 years gave Georgia what turned out to be a very special gift. It was a small cloth doll, wearing a velvet dress. She is called Nancy.

Georgia and her transitional objects

Georgia becomes very attached to Nancy and soon will not go anywhere without her dummy and the doll. Dummy and Nancy become 'transitional objects' which she uses for comfort and security (Winnicott, 1975). Sometimes young children use inanimate objects such as blankets, cuddly toys or dummies for comfort in new situations or at times when they separate from the people to whom they are closely attached (Bowlby, 1991). It is as though having a familiar and loved object to cuddle helps Georgia to feel safe.

Georgia uses role play

Georgia's dad leaves his firm and gets another job in a different toy company. Although she does not ever meet his new boss, Kai, Georgia incorporates him into her role play. This helps her to understand who Kai is. When she is 2 years 11 months Georgia chats to her grandmother:

> **Grandmother:** *'I must get ready for work soon.'*
> **Georgia:** *'Work . . . me been to daddy's work.'*
> **Gran:** *'Who was there?'*
> **Georgia:** *'Bill.'*
> **Gran:** *'Anyone else?'*
> **Georgia:** *'Kai's called the boss.'*
>
> *Later Eloise gave Georgia a small case with some things in. She carried it around for a while and then said 'This is a briefcase . . . me be the boss too.'*
> (Parent diary)

Before Georgia was born

As well as being interested in people who she does not see but hears about, Georgia is also intrigued by family events that took place before her birth. At 2 years 5 months her favourite story is about the car crash her parents were involved in before she was born.

Grandmother: *'She wants to know what happened when Ian and Colette had a car accident. She can relate the story and likes to see the newspaper cutting of the crashed car. When they are out in the car, she says she is looking for the car that was involved in the accident. (Her mum explains that both cars were so broken they could not be used again).'*

Looking back with Georgia's parents

Georgia's parents and her nursery worker talk together about her when she was 2 to 3 years old. Her mum describes Georgia as a 'people person'.

Mum: *'She is always interested in people and in what they are doing. Even on holiday she always seems to link up with other children. They are often older than her.'*

Her mum believes that at 2 or 3 years old Georgia played with children who were several years older because 'they let her have her own way'. The twins, for example, 'were into looking after babies'. Georgia could fulfil a role in their games. Schaffer (1996) says that for cognitive (intellectual) change to occur, although there is no conclusive evidence yet, it seems that 'at younger ages children require a person of greater competence than themselves' while 'later on, a person of equal or even lesser capability will suffice'. Gradually Georgia begins to play with children nearer her own age.

Mum: *'She began playing with Samantha at around three or four and Big Emma at five or six.'*

Georgia's dad sees Georgia at 7 years as being very like the twins (Jennifer and Amy) were at the same age.

Dad: *'Georgia likes older girls or babies – she loves to play with James' baby cousin.'*

The other children that Georgia meets are the children of her parents' friends, some of whom begin playgroup and nursery when she does.

How people affect Georgia's development and learning

It is difficult to work out whether Georgia was born 'a people person' or becomes 'a people person' because of her early experiences. Research into temperament indicates that some children tend to be high on 'sociability' (Buss and Plomin, 1984). It appears that the important factor is the 'goodness of fit between the child's temperament and the context in which the child finds itself' (Oates, 1994). Georgia, who is sociable, seeks out and reacts positively towards other people. If people respond to this sociability, then Georgia will continue to be sociable.

The 'goodness of fit', in this case, is between Georgia's personality and the context in which she has the opportunity to get to know the range of people of varying ages and interests.

Her attachments to the people in the close as well as to her extended family, offer her a great deal of stability and security. This is a predictable environment for her and one that stays the same throughout other changes in her life. She is 7 years old and the same people are all still living there.

Georgia and her role models

Georgia gets ideas about what she wants to do from the people she knows. She seems to build up a story of her own possible future by using people she admires as role models. For example, Jennifer and Amy have been going to gymnastics for as long as Georgia has known them. She spends a lot of time trying out handstands and other movements that they have been practising in the close. Georgia begins a gymnastic class when she is old enough.

At 2 years 11 months Georgia speaks confidently about going to school.

> **Georgia:** *'When me five or six me go to school with Amy, Jennifer and Nicola, same school.'*

Georgia seems to choose others to play with when she and they are at a similar stage developmentally, or when they have shared interests. She and Samantha gravitate towards one another when Georgia is 3 years 6 months and Samantha is 5 years. Both are interested in drawing and writing. The three months between Georgia and James seems a big age gap until both children are 4 years old. He is physically taller than her and both children are riding two wheeled bicycles. They swap bikes and race against each other.

WHERE GEORGIA GOES

Georgia's mum likes to go out each day so, over time, she adopts a routine. She might go to her local under-fives centre (to attend groups, baby massage or drop-in), visit or be visited by friends, shop or go to see Georgia's grandparents. At weekends Georgia might be taken to the zoo, a local park or go swimming.

Before Harry is born, the family go on holiday to Tenerife and twice to Majorca. The holiday photographs show that on each holiday Georgia makes friends with other children and adults.

Looking back with Georgia's parents

Her dad cannot remember Georgia having particular preferences for places. He can remember that she 'loved Wicksteed Park, especially the swings. We used to go there every week.' When her brother is being born, her grandmother and uncle take her to Wicksteed Park and push her on the swings because they know they can keep her happy and amused there.

> **Mum:** *'She liked going to people's houses. She liked being with people.' I never worried about what she would be like in public – she was always good.'*

(Her mum explains that Georgia was always well-behaved and happy when she was with people outside her immediate family.)

Georgia's parents take her swimming occasionally.

> **Dad:** *'She always loved the water – she spent half of her life in the bath or at the sink.'*

How going places affects Georgia's development and learning

Going to the shops
When Georgia is around 2 years, she spends a lot of time playing with money, dishing out 'tickets' and playing shops. Although shopping, to her parents, is routine, Georgia seems to learn a great deal from her trips to the shops. Her early understanding that 20p buys her a ride on a toy train at the supermarket, prompts her to call a 20p coin a 'choo choo'.

Georgia's dad says that she loves playing with and in water!

Going to the creche

When her mum attends groups at the under-fives centre, Georgia goes to the creche. This gives her a new experience with different people, away from the familiarity of the close. Often she is with children she knows well – the children of her parents' friends. Attending creche helps Georgia to trust that her mum will come back for her and also helps her to learn a sense of what a 'couple of hours' means. A creche session is one and a half hours long.

Going to the playgroup

Several of the children from the creche start playgroup at the same time. Georgia is familiar with the physical layout of the building, so 'playgroup' is not a strange, new place – it is very close to the creche which she knows well. Her transition to playgroup seems to be smooth, possibly because she understands what happens and knows several other children. Georgia begins attending playgroup five mornings a week when she is 2 years 7 months. Each session lasts 2 hours.

GEORGIA'S PLAY

Georgia's interests

Georgia is 3 years 7 months when she starts nursery. The chart below shows her main interests at home and at nursery and is based on observations made around the time of starting nursery.

WHAT GEORGIA DOES	WHO WITH?	WHERE?
Plays on the rocking-horse	Alone or with Harry	Nursery
Playing with water	Alone or with children outside	Home
Using dough or clay	Alongside peers	Nursery
Playing with dolls	Alone or with Jennifer and Harry	Home
Taking part in role play	With Big Emma or Harry	Home
	With Steph, Laura and Harry or with peers	Family Room* Nursery (occasionally)
Drawing and writing	With Samantha or older children	Home
	Alongside peers or adults	Nursery
Listening to stories	With adults	Home
	With adults	Nursery
Using the computer	With adults	Grandparents' house
	With adults	Nursery
Painting	With older children or Harry	Home
	With peers	Nursery
Sticking/collage	Alone or with Harry	Home
	With Steph, Emma and Laura	Nursery
Building/using construction materials	Alone or with Harry	Home or at grandparents'
	Alone or with Steph	Nursery
Woodwork	Alongside adult	Nursery

WHAT GEORGIA DOES	WHO WITH?	WHERE?
Playing outside with bikes, trailers and climbing equipment	Children in close	Home
	Steph, Laura and others	Nursery

* The Family Room is a room at the under-fives centre. Families can drop in and stay as long as they wish. There are toys for the children, drinks and sometimes lunch.

While this table cannot give a completely comprehensive list, it does show where Georgia makes links between what she does at home and what she chooses at nursery.

Shortly after Georgia starts nursery, her mum begins evening work. This change knocks her confidence a little – Chapter 6 describes how Georgia deals with change and uncertainty.

Looking back with Georgia's Parents

Different things to do
Georgia's dad is struck by his observation that she seems to do 'different things in different places'. He wonders '. . . maybe she categorised them.'

> **Mum:** *'Was she using nursery for things she did not get at home or in the Family Room?'*

Different people
Role play seems to be the predominant play both at home and in the Family Room, where the children who play together are from a wider age range. Often games are initiated by the older children in the group. Maybe at home in the close, older children initiate games, and in the Family Room, Georgia, as one of the older children there, can take the lead? Her mum is certain that '. . . she does get something from playing with older children.' The size of the group may influence what happens. In the close, there are usually five or six children playing together. In the Family Room, it is probably about the same number or less. In nursery, about 35 children attend each session. Although there is plenty of space and 'cosy areas' have been created in which children can develop more complex play, (Bruner, 1980), Georgia is new to nursery and may feel more secure near an adult. It may not be a coincidence that she frequently chooses to have stories and to go on the computer, as each guarantees having an adult alongside.

When Georgia does move away from adults, she is usually alongside Steph and other children she knows from creche and playgroup.

Making links

When Georgia plays with blocks she seems prepared to build alone or with a partner. Her dad recalls that, as a baby, Georgia played for long periods with her babywalker and blocks. She may find playing with maple blocks intrinsically more satisfying than other lone activities.

Bringing experiences from home to nursery

Trying new experiences

Getting to know the people and how things work seems to be important for Georgia at nursery. She is not always prepared to try out something new without first observing what happens. For example, although she has been massaged by her mum since she was a baby, when foot massage is offered in nursery, she is most comfortable observing Steph having her feet massaged before taking part herself.

Learning the system

Georgia very quickly understands the system for getting a turn on the computer. There is a book in which an adult (or the child) writes the child's name. You are called when it is your turn. Adults try not to limit children's learning by deciding how long each child needs on the computer. Georgia understands taking turns. Some of the street games in which Georgia has participated use turn-taking. Taking turns physically precedes the abstract idea of being in a queue which is written down in a book.

Going out on the minibus is organised in a similar way. Adults or children write down the names of the children who want to go out on the minibus in a special book. If your name is down and there is not room, you get a turn the next time there is a trip. Again, Georgia very quickly works out the system.

Having a laugh

Although Georgia likes to be alongside familiar people and to know what is going to happen next, one of the exciting things about people is their unpredictability. Georgia is also excited and attracted by this unpredictability. She likes to watch and sometimes do things which are slightly risque. She loves to have fun and to laugh raucously. Whereas at home she might be instigating the laughter by deliberately saying something funny or humorous, at nursery she is more likely to be watching and listening.

Georgia's Family Worker

Georgia's nursery has a Key Worker system (Whalley, 1997). Alison is Georgia's Family Worker. Alison visited Georgia and her family at home prior to Georgia starting nursery and Georgia is in Alison's 'group' at nursery. Once Georgia has established that there is a regular, predictable routine whereby she joins her Family Group for the last 20 minutes each day, she begins to choose to go with different Family Workers. This is a sign of being settled and wanting to explore what happens in other Family Groups.

Different equipment

There is a great deal of equipment out of doors at nursery for children to extend their development and learning (there are co-operative vehicles and trailers as well as climbing equipment). Georgia makes good use of the equipment. She enjoys the trailers at nursery so much that her parents buy her a trailer for Christmas.

Georgia's transition from home to nursery is a gradual one, involving brief sessions spent in creche, then a year in playgroup before joining nursery. During her year at playgroup Georgia tries to master the monkey bars (in the playgroup playground). This is adjacent to the nursery playground and is used by nursery children and staff too. Georgia is able to continue her strive to master the monkey bars while she is at nursery.

Getting to grips with the monkey bars

Summary

- When Georgia is born, her family live in a small, intimate close.

- Georgia gets to know several people who are important to her.

- Georgia's transition to nursery is via creche and playgroup, which are situated on the same site.

We have been introduced to Georgia and the people who are important to her. In the next chapter we shall begin to look at her from many different angles – through different theories and how what she does links with research. We shall begin to see how we can assess and evaluate what she is learning and the implications this has for the way we work with children and their families.

2 EARLY CHILDHOOD EDUCATION, CARE AND TRADITIONS

'I dunno,' Arthur said, 'I forgot what I was taught. I only remember what I've learnt.'
(White in Cohen, 1993)

Not enough attention is paid to how children learn most effectively and consequently how teachers can teach most effectively.
(Athey, 1990)

Whether the 'teacher' is a parent, health visitor or classroom assistant, their aim is generally to help children to learn effectively. The ways in which adults have a shared view of children and the childhood they want for them, may be a suitable starting point for thinking about Georgia and how she learns. Learning and teaching are inextricably linked together.

- **Different views of Georgia** – looking at Georgia through the theories of Piaget, Vygotsky and in the light of current research of Laevers, Goleman, Gardner and neuroscientists.

- **Assessing what Georgia is learning** – seeing her as a whole child, listening to her parents and gathering narrative observations of her spontaneous actions.

- **Analysing observations** – by using AIRSS (autonomy, involvement, relationships, schemas and strategies: Arnold, 1997) or by using traditional subject areas.

- **Staff training** – linking theory and practice, developing skills in gathering and analysing narrative observations.

VIEWS OF EARLY CHILDHOOD

We can look at Georgia through various different theoretical perspectives. Both Piaget and Vygotsky were born in 1896, so their's are not new ideas. However, aspects of their original theories, which we can use in trying to understand Georgia's learning, continue to influence and to be developed by others.

Jean Piaget

Piaget had a background in genetic epistemology (how knowledge grows), so it is not surprising that he began his investigations by observing his own three children in naturally occurring situations, in exactly the same way that he might have observed shellfish in their natural habitats! In his early work, Piaget did not set up experimental situations. These early naturalistic observations were the basis for formulating his theories.

Piaget's major ideas

1   Knowledge is constructed by the learner.
2   Learners pass through stages of development.
3   Children display **schemas** (or patterns of behaviour) that are generalisable.
4   Development from one stage to the next occurs through processes that Piaget calls **assimilation**, **accommodation** and **equilibration**.

Knowledge is constructed by the learner

Piaget would argue that Georgia's knowledge is not necessarily transmitted from someone else to her. Georgia's learning is an *active* process during which she constructs knowledge from her own firsthand experiences. When Georgia asks a question about something she desperately wants to understand, it is not simply a question of her parents responding to her question and transferring their knowledge to her. For example, when Georgia is 2 years 7 months, she watches some rabbits in a hutch outside. It is pouring with rain and she says repeatedly, 'Rabbits get wet?'. Her mum explains that they are inside the hutch and the rain does not go through. It is not until months later, that Georgia displays her understanding of *how* the roof protects the rabbits from the rain. We see how she does this in the next section.

Learners pass through stages of development

Piaget is famous for his stage theory. Georgia, he would suggest, passes through stages of development and can only function at a higher level when she reaches that particular stage of development. He would say that her intellectual development is taking place in four major periods:

1   **Sensorimotor** (from birth to 2 years).
2   **Preoperational** (2 to 7 years).
3   **Concrete operational** (7 to 11 years).
4   **Formal operational** (11 years and above).

Piaget suggests these as average ages at which transformations in intellectual functioning might take place. Piaget would expect Georgia to be active in constructing ideas through her own actions, which she later internalises as thoughts (Donaldson, 1978). Continuing the story above, at 2 years 7 months Georgia can see heavy rain pouring down and rabbits outside of the building in which she is physically dry. In order to understand the concept of covering in order to protect, Georgia actively explores getting wet and covering, or **enveloping**. Her development plays a role, in that she becomes able to combine more than one idea together at a time. Georgia also becomes interested in cause and effect, so pays attention to *how* the rabbits are protected from the heavy rain.

The ages at which Piaget suggested children pass through the four stages have been strongly challenged (Bruce, 1997). Donaldson's discovery that the problems children are presented with must be embedded in the context of their lives, was a real breakthrough and challenged all early childhood educators to consider children's knowledge in the context of their real lives (Donaldson, 1978). *makes difference if had input from parents not really nature V nuture.*

Children display schemas that are generalisable

Piaget's theory suggests that Georgia explores the world by trying out patterns of behaviour or schemas on everything she meets in her environment. She generalises new information into her current schemas. Schemas become co-ordinated into increasingly complex combinations. For example, we might consider Georgia's concern that the rabbits are getting wet from the heavy rain. Subsequently Georgia spends several months exploring an envelopment schema, covering objects with various materials in order to see what happens. Finally she understands how covering the rabbits with the roof protects them from the rain. Then Georgia begins to notice how a gap in the covering allows some materials to go through the covering. She is sensitive to and explores ideas about going through and is able to adapt her current schema to include these new ideas (see Chapter Five for a more extensive explanation).

An aside – schemas

Piaget's research on schemas has been developed by a number of people in the last 30 years (Nicholls, 1986; Athey, 1990; Arnold, 1990; Shaw, 1991; Nutbrown, 1994; Matthews, 1994; Meade with Cubey, 1995; Rice, 1996; Arnold, 1997; Bruce, 1997). Schemas are patterns of behaviour which children try out on everything they come across in their environment. Bruce (1997) says that, *use that*

Schemas are part of human development, from birth to death, but they are not in a constant state. They are always adjusting and changing in the light of experience. This is why they are such powerful learning mechanisms.

When we are trying to identify children's schemas it is helpful to look at current research findings. In a study of four children over 18 months, the aspects of schemas observed in all four children were ranked from the most to least frequently observed (Arnold, 1997). Each schema is accompanied by a brief explanation:

Most frequently observed

- **Envelopment** – enveloping, covering or surrounding oneself, an object or a space.

- **Trajectory** – moving in or representing straight lines, arcs or curves.

- **Enclosure** – enclosing oneself, an object or a space.

- **Transporting** – carrying objects or being carried from one place to another.

- **Connection** – an interest in connecting themselves to objects and objects to each other.

- **Rotation** – turning, twisting or rolling oneself or objects in the environment around.

- **Going through a boundary** – causing oneself or material or an object to go through a boundary and emerge at the other side.

- **Oblique trajectory** – moving in, using or drawing oblique lines.

- **Containment** – putting materials inside an object which is capable of containing them.

- **Transformation** – transforming oneself by dressing differently or being interested in changes in state.

Least frequently observed
Altogether 41 aspects of schemas were observed, but many were combinations and co-ordinations of those listed above.
   Schemas are explored in different ways. They can be **dynamic** (moving

like a piece of video) or **configurative** (still like a photograph) (Bruce, 1997). They also function at different levels:

- **Sensori motor level** – through the senses, actions and movement.

- **Symbolic level** – making something stand for something else.

- **Cause and effect** – sometimes called **functional dependency** (if I do this, then that will happen).

- **Abstract thought level** – when there is increasing understanding of reversibility and transformations and a co-ordinated understanding of these.

The advantage of using schemas as observation tools is that we do not need to know the theory in great depth to begin spotting patterns of behaviour and extending our provision accordingly. We can begin by reflecting back to children what we have observed. For example, Georgia's Family Worker might say to her, 'I see you are covering your babies to keep them warm and dry'. We could offer her different coverings and watch what she does with them.

Assimilation, accommodation and equilibration

Piaget's explanation is that, as Georgia tries out her current schemas on objects in the environment, she assimilates new content into her current structures. When she comes across something that will not fit into that structure, she accommodates the new information by changing the structure and, in doing this, reaches a kind of equilibrium. For example, when Georgia becomes 3 years old, she counts 1, 2, 3 and says she is 3. The number '3' is a label. Her age is, to her, synonymous with her name. She assimilates the information that she 'is 3' into her current 'naming of age' structure. Some months later, her friend Stephanie, has her fourth birthday. Georgia is concerned and puzzled that her friend becomes 4 years old before her. Her current 'naming of age' structure does not explain why her friend suddenly has a different age label to hers. She frequently asks why Steph is 4 years old before she is. Her mum explains many times that Steph was born before she was and that Steph has lived longer. Georgia asks the same questions repeatedly over several months. Finally she accommodates the information by changing her structure from a 'naming of age' structure to include a 'lived age' structure and reaches a sort of equilibrium or balance.

The urge to explore the world in this way is a biological one. The content or experiences through which Georgia learns, depends on the culture or community in which she is born and raised. The concern with the influence of culture is Vygotskerian.

Lev Vygotsky

Vygotsky was the second of eight children born to a Jewish family in Russia in 1896. It is probably not a coincidence that his main concern was with the social context of learning.

Vygotsky's major theories

1   Children develop by interacting with other people.
2   There is a **zone of proximal** (or **potential**) **development** within which children can function at a higher level with help.
3   Children develop **spontaneous concepts** before learning **scientific concepts**.

Children develop by interacting with other people

Vygotsky believes that social interaction is the force that drives intellectual development. He sees social interaction as the source of development. He would say that Georgia 'internalises' the conversations she has had with others (Flanagan, 1996). At first Georgia speaks to herself out loud, but eventually, this kind of 'self-talk' becomes her thinking. An example of this is Georgia's early repetition of the sorts of things she has heard her parents say in shops and at the park. During her own play, she repeats these phrases for example, 'Pay the man', 'pay 60' and 'I don't know if I've got 60'. Through using these phrases in her play she converts them into her own language, which she can use to think.

There is a zone of proximal development

Vygotsky puts a great deal of emphasis on the role of the adult or older child who, by instruction and support, guides children to achieve at a higher level than they would alone. The zone of proximal development (Moll, 1990) is the area of nearest potential development for a child. So, with help and guidance, Georgia can tackle things that are a challenge to her, but that are still connected to her earlier learning. When Georgia is interested in size and fit, her mum helps her to measure a picture for framing. Gradually, over time, Georgia learns to do this accurately without help.

Spontaneous and scientific concepts

Vygotsky puts forward the idea that concepts develop as a result of children's experience in the world. He refers to these as spontaneous concepts. He emphasises that scientific concepts must be taught. So, only when Georgia has learned through experience and been taught systematically will she gain **true concepts** (Au, 1990). Vygotsky believes that instruction precedes development (Vygotsky, 1962; Daniels, 1996). For example, when Georgia looks at books about pregnancy and her parents explain what will happen when her sibling is born, she is receiving 'instruction'. But Georgia does not grasp the full concept until she has experienced related spontaneous concepts and is developmentally mature enough to understand how a baby is born. (See Chapter Five for a full explanation of Georgia's explorations.)

Piaget and Vygotsky look at different aspects of learning and teaching. The theories they each develop are not necessarily in opposition to each other. Piaget leaves us with the view of Georgia as a **lone explorer** constructing knowledge for herself. He is not explicit about the role of her parents, teachers or care workers. The danger in taking a Piagetian approach is in being too laissez-faire, that is, structuring the environment with resources but paying little attention to the interactions with and between Georgia and other children within that environment.

Vygotsky's emphasis leaves us with the view of Georgia as a **social being** who learns through her interactions with other people. The danger in taking a Vygotskerian approach is that the adult may dominate with ideas and instruction. This is particularly inappropriate during the early years when Georgia needs to initiate her own learning (Bruce, 1997).

Other than the fundamentally different ideas, that 'actions become thoughts' (Piaget) and 'conversations become thoughts' (Vygotsky), we can apply both Piagetian theory and Vygotskerian theory to our work with Georgia. In fact, using aspects of both theories to help her learn creates a balanced approach. We need to remember that both actions and conversations are important to Georgia as she learns. Bruce (1997) supports the idea that 'there are two aspects of a child's development: the **biological path** and the **socio-cultural path**.'

Current views of early childhood

In this section we shall see how the work of Ferre Laevers, Daniel Goleman, Howard Gardner and recent research by several neuroscientists can help us to make sense of Georgia's learning.

Ferre Laevers
Laevers has been working at Leuven University in Belgium for more than 20 years on a 'process–oriented child monitoring system' (Laevers, 1995). In carrying out this work, and drawing on the theories of both Piaget and

Vygotsky, Laevers has developed two tools for monitoring how and when children are developing and learning. Laevers says:

For development to occur, children need to be high on 'emotional well-being' and high on 'involvement'.

Emotional well-being

Well-being can be characterised by:

- openness and receptivity
- flexibility
- self-confidence and self-esteem
- assertiveness
- vitality
- relaxation and inner peace
- enjoyment
- the child feeling connected and in touch with herself.

Involvement

Signs of involvement are:

- concentration
- energy
- complexity and creativity
- facial expression and composure
- persistence
- precision
- reaction time
- verbal expression
- satisfaction.

Involvement is about the *quality* of activity not the *contents* (Laevers, 1997). Highly involved human beings 'feel intrinsically motivated to carry on because the activity falls in with what they want to learn and know, i.e. their exploratory drive . . .' Linked with the ability to be highly involved intellectually, is the need for emotional well-being. The idea of emotional well-being as a concern of teachers, nursery nurses, parents or health visitors is not a new one, but has recently been highlighted in the work of Laevers and also of Daniel Goleman in the USA.

Daniel Goleman

Daniel Goleman emphasises 'emotional intelligence'. He would focus on the all round ability of Georgia, particularly in terms of her knowing 'how to learn'. He says,

> . . . *success in school depends to a surprising extent on emotional characteristics formed in the years before a child enters school.*
> (Goleman, 1996)

Goleman lists seven ingredients that contribute to a child's ability to know how to learn:

- Confidence
- Curiosity
- Intentionality
- Self-control
- Relatedness
- Capacity to communicate
- Co-operativeness.

Georgia's parents intuitively know that it is important for her to become independent and to learn to make friends in her early years. Starting nursery or going into childcare provision is, as it is for many children, her first step on the road to becoming independent.

Howard Gardner

Gardner has put forward a theory of multiple intelligences. His theory is that there are at least 'seven ways of knowing the world' (Gardner, 1991). People learn in many different ways and may favour one way rather than another. The learning paths he has identified operate through:

- language

- logical, mathematical representation

- spatial representation

- musical thinking

- the use of the body to solve problems or to make things

- an understanding of other individuals

- an understanding of ourselves.

Gardner and his colleagues have devised an educational approach called **Project Spectrum**, which we can use to identify Georgia's talents and abilities and to build on them.

> *In a Spectrum classroom, children are surrounded each day by rich and engaging materials . . . there is a naturalist's corner . . . a storytelling area . . . a building corner . . . Numerous other intelligences, and combinations of intelligences, are tapped in the remaining dozen areas and activities . . .*
> (Gardner, 1991)

The Spectrum team feel it is important for children to be alongside adults or older children. Georgia would benefit from such an environment. It would encourage her to be both a Piagetian 'explorer' and a Vygotskerian 'apprentice'.

Recent research by neuroscientists

The importance of the early years has recently been confirmed by the findings of a number of neuroscientists. The discovery that the brain develops at an alarming rate shortly after birth, means that this 'sensitive period' is a time when all children, including Georgia, need stimulation (Barnes, 1995). At birth, children's brains have a surplus of neurons and only those that make connections (or synapses) survive.

> *. . . the number of connections (synapses) between neurons . . . are thought to be crucial to the integrity and complexity of information processing in the brain.*
> (Oates, 1994)

Babies are born with great potential for learning and it is the environment in which they are brought up that provides the stimulation for what they learn.

Susan Greenfield (1997) says,

> *In the brain, then, activity and growth go hand in hand: it is not only a question of 'use it or lose it' but 'use it as much as you can'.*

Nash (1997) confirms the need for young children to explore, when she says,

> *Rich experiences really do produce rich brains.*

ASSESSING WHAT GEORGIA IS LEARNING

Our nets define what we will catch.
(Eisner, 1985)

The views of childhood that we have been considering seem to indicate that Georgia is a unique individual, who learns in many different ways. Our way of assessing her learning needs to be equally comprehensive. In fact, Georgia makes this a fairly straightforward task. She does not respond well to experiments, and observation of her actions in the normal course of events seems to be the only option.

Observing Georgia

We (as workers and parents) could decide to focus on particular aspects of Georgia's learning, for example, her conversation or what she does out of doors. We would make notes whenever conversation or outdoor play occurred and, over time, assess aspects of Georgia's development or learning through her language or how she plays out of doors. However, by restricting our focus, we would miss a great deal of her development and learning. The essence of a **whole child approach** is that we really do not know what, how or where Georgia is going to develop and learn. So, we decide to record *whatever* Georgia does while we are observing, without analysing what we see. This means recording, as *accurately* and *precisely* as possible, without making judgements, the actions and language we observe and hear. There are several tools which we could choose to do this, for example:

- paper and pen
- dictaphone

- camera

- video camera.

Each tool has advantages and disadvantages and may tell us something different.

Pen and paper

There is often too much happening to record in any detail – we may end up writing down only the essence of what we see. Conversations, in particular, are so fast that it is difficult to record everything said. As an observer, we will notice other things happening which may be significant. It can be an advantage to know what else is happening in the area surrounding the child who is the target of our observation. Events nearby can have an influence on what a target child does. Alternatively, if they have no influence, we can ignore the information.

Dictaphone

A dictaphone is useful, but if we are physically close to Georgia, she may become interested in the dictaphone. (This may be true of any technological tool.) In one sense this does not matter, as the dictaphone can be regarded as fresh stimulation. Therefore, whatever Georgia does or says in connection with the tool, becomes the focus.

Camera

A camera takes one or several snapshots, which just capture a moment in time unless we add contextual information.

Video

A video camera preserves what happens, but all we capture is what is in focus at the time of recording. There is, however, the possibility of using the video material as a stimulus to help Georgia and her parents recall what else happened both on and off camera. A set of video stills can illustrate a process.

Gathering information over time provides the raw data to make a formative assessment of Georgia's development and learning. The data, in all sorts of different forms, can be collected by professionals and by her parents. Georgia's Family Workers are trying to make connections with Georgia's home context, which makes learning at nursery more meaningful for her. Her parents are trying to ensure the best education and care for Georgia and their contribution to recordkeeping will make nursery better for her.

A set of video stills can illustrate a process

Looking back with Georgia's parents

Georgia's parents are the true experts on Georgia (Whalley, 1997). It is, therefore, crucial that professionals working with Georgia listen to her parents. Parents and workers can share information about what she says and does, during informal daily chats. It will also be important for professionals working with Georgia to ask her parents for more detailed feedback about what she does at home. Georgia's parents kept a diary for 18 months of some of her actions and language at home.

What to record

One difficulty is what to record. Georgia's parents were asked to gather a **time sample** (Webb, 1975), that is, to record whatever happened during a 20 minute period, once a week. They were also asked to record anything they found 'curious' or 'interesting' that Georgia did or said. The information her parents recorded, along with the record of what and who Georgia played with at nursery formed the basis for further discussion and analysis.

Involving parents

More recently, as part of the *Parents' Involvement in Their Children's Learning* project (funded by the Esmee Fairbairn Trust) parents are being asked to write down or video what their children are doing when they are 'deeply involved' (Laevers, 1995). This project seems to be capturing the essence of what children are interested in and motivated to do at home.

Piaget's early work on schemas was superbly developed during the 1970s by the Froebel team who were working in partnership with parents. Identifying children's schemas and providing content and language to extend each identified 'form' or schema was the main focus of the project (Athey, 1990).

Athey reports.

> *A genuine 'open-ended' type of enquiry was encouraged with everyone working together to find patterns of cognition.*

If a truly collaborative approach is fostered, then there will be benefits for Georgia, her parents and the professionals who work with her. Athey believes 'the greatest benefit to teachers in working with parents is the spur towards making their own pedagogy more conscious and explicit'. The process of sharing information about learning, helps professionals to articulate with more clarity their ideas about teaching Georgia.

When we listen to Georgia's parents, we not only gain valuable information about the place, events and the people with whom she spends most of her time, but we also convey hidden messages about valuing each parent's contribution to her education. Acknowledging and being interested in Georgia's experiences at home means being interested in her whole educational experience.

Gathering narrative observations

There is a long tradition of gathering narrative observations in early childhood education (Bartholomew and Bruce, 1993). Bartholomew and Bruce say that,

> *Narrative records keep emphasising strengths, while pre-structured record forms can quickly lead to a focus on weakness, failure and 'can't do'.*

Observations such as those made by Piaget (1951) of his own children give us a glimpse of the rich complexity of what happened in their learning and development.

For example,

> *At 3 [years]; 3 [months] J asked her first question about birth in the shape of a query as to where L came from (L was 1 [year]; 8 [months]):* 'Daddy where did you find the little baby in a cradle? – *Which baby?* – Nonette *(i.e. L).'* My *reply was simply that mummy and daddy had given her a little sister. At 3 [years]; 6 [months] she touched her grandmother's eyes, nose, etc., and said to her:* 'Is that how grannies are made? Did you make yourself?' *And later:* 'Did she make herself? What made her?' *The same evening, when looking at L:* 'Why do they have little hands, little teeth, little eyes, a little mouth?'

Piaget's concern is to discover what J is thinking about and wanting to discover. He makes links, over time, between her spontaneous enquiries.

Susan Isaacs ran an experimental school in Cambridge for 3 years during the 1920s. Her work continues to influence ideas about early childhood education today. She and her staff kept extensive narrative records of what happened in the Malting House School and some of the parents kept records of what their children did and said at home. This is a sample (1966):

> *17.2.25. One of the children stood on a chair, and said, 'I'm taller than you' to the others. They all of them then got on chairs, and Frank and Christopher both said they were taller than Dan. Dan [3 years, 9 months] then said to Frank, 'Yes we* are *taller than Christopher, aren't we?' (Dan being much the smallest of the three.)*

Susan Isaacs' concern was to encourage the children in her school to develop their own interests in the fullest way.

Gathering observations in this way is like being a reporter who writes down or films whatever happens. The focus is on the *here* and *now*.

ANALYSING OBSERVATIONS

> *But most by numbers judge a poet's song:*
> *And smooth or rough with them, is right or wrong:*
> (Pope, 1985)

By analysing observations we show the progress that Georgia makes in her learning. At this point, we may want to consider **normative development** or what is considered 'normal' for most children of the same age (Oates, 1994). We must not allow normative goals to limit what Georgia does and what we record about Georgia's learning. There can be a tendency, when considering norms to see them as *outcomes to be achieved* and to judge what Georgia does as right or wrong in this context. Achievement at any given moment must not be confused with *ability*. A full record gathered over time gives us information about Georgia's experience of specific subject areas, as well as information about her particular interests and her 'dispositions', such as curiosity (Katz, 1993). One observation gives us only a limited amount of information about Georgia. It is a sort of snapshot of her. However, even a snapshot can be analysed in more than one way. This section shows how we can analyse one day's observation from home in two different ways.

> *Georgia (3 years 7 months) has a roll of sellotape which she has really enjoyed playing with lately. She has been cutting off different length strips and sticking them, randomly, onto paper.*
>
> *Georgia has been jumping up trying to reach things – still doing things with tiptoes and without. A couple of times, she has also got inside a pillowcase and jumped out.*
>
> *Georgia is still <u>obsessed</u> with time – how long it takes to get places – how long until something happens. It does not seem to matter whether it is a long time or not. She is already picking the watch she wants from Argos and trying to tell the time.*
> (Parent Diary)

Introducing analysis according to AIRSS

AIRSS stands for: **Autonomy, Involvement, Relationships, Schemas** and **Strategies** (Arnold, 1997).

The AIRSS tool has evolved from considering Georgia's learning and examines:

- how Georgia chooses and acts independently, therefore displaying self-government or autonomy (Dweck and Leggett, 1988; Whalley, 1994)

- Georgia's inner state of involvement (Laevers, 1995)

- who she interacts with and the nature of the interactions or relationships (Pollard, 1996)

- Georgia's repeated patterns of behaviour or schema (Piaget, 1951; Athey, 1990)

- how she approaches new situations and people. These are her strategies (Nisbet and Shucksmith, 1986; Pollard, 1996)

Autonomy

Georgia seems to be *choosing* to do what she does with the sellotape, as well as *choosing* which watch she wants from Argos. She has decided which materials to play with and how she uses the materials.

Involvement

The tone of the parent observations indicates Georgia's *intrinsic motivation* to use sellotape, jump to reach and ask questions about time.

Relationships

There is no record of play with peers although the observations indicate a good relationship with her parents. (That is, she is able to explore and practise as well as ask questions.)

Schemas

All three observations indicate an interest in trajectory behaviour (see page 22). In the first, she is using different *lengths* of sellotape; in the second, she is using her body to reach an increased *height*; in the third she is interested in the *duration* or *length of time* until something happens. Georgia is using her trajectory schema at a sensori-motor level (see page 23) when cutting the sellotape and jumping. She is using her trajectory schema at a cause and effect level when jumping to reach, that is, 'if I jump higher, I will reach a higher point'. She is moving towards Abstract thought level when asking about duration of time (understanding the duration of time involves holding in mind a sort of line from one point in time to another point in time). Like Athey in some of the observations gathered in the Froebel project, in the absence of clues from Georgia, we cannot tell whether or not she is functioning at a symbolic level (making one thing stand for another).

Strategies

Georgia seems to be using *spontaneous activity* and *asking questions* as her two main strategies.

Analysis according to the traditional subject areas

Communication, language and literacy

Georgia is asking questions to gain information about time. She is interested in cracking the code which will enable her to read number symbols and tell the time.

Mathematical understanding

Georgia is exploring ideas about length, height and duration. Her parents have not included the specific language she uses, although she is involved in practical activities that are mathematical. She is asking questions about time and distance.

Scientific understanding

Georgia is exploring the properties of matter, in this case the stickiness of the sellotape. She displays scientific curiosity (a disposition which helps her to learn) in relation to understanding time as a concept.

Personal and social development

Georgia is eager to explore and initiate new ideas. This is indicated by her enjoyment when playing with the sellotape, her pursuit of jumping up and her obsession with time.

IMPLICATIONS FOR STAFF TRAINING

As professionals and parents, we may find it helpful to discuss what kind of childhood we want for the children in our care. Most adults have had some positive experiences and some less positive to inform their views. The focus for a parents' evening could be a discussion of 'The Education We Want for Our Children'.

Stating our principles

It is helpful to examine our principles, that is, what we and the parents of the children we work with, see as important. Bruce et al (1995) say that it is 'when theory and educational principles interact' that 'practice makes progress'. It is a question of looking out at the world and considering the theories and practice of others, whilst making explicit our own underlying principles about young children.

There are several ways of finding out about current theories:

- reading education, health and research journals

- visiting other settings in this country and abroad

- going on courses and to conferences

- undertaking education or training which links with the work that we do.

Sharing ideas

Within a group of staff, it can be quite difficult for any one individual to exert influence on the group to effect changes in practice. The vision needs to be a shared one. Therefore, inviting a trainer to work with the group, might be the most effective way of improving practice.

It is increasingly recognised that some regular non-contact time is central to work in any early years setting if quality is to be maintained. Time in which to analyse and discuss observations and to make home visits is an important part of the work.

Home visiting forms a major part of some professionals' work while others might need training to undertake home visits. For example, health visitors carry out most of their work in family homes, whereas some teachers might find it daunting to visit children at home. Some cross fertilisation of ideas might be productive. Teachers might feel confident to share their ideas about theories and principles of education with health visitors, while health visitors might be able to offer reassurance and support with home visiting. Practitioners, who have undertaken CACHE/NNEB training, usually have a good grounding in writing observations. This is a skill which can be shared with other colleagues and parents.

Gathering narrative observations

Making good observations is a skill that we can improve by practising. Showing every written observation of Georgia to her parents, not only improves our expressive writing skills, but raises out awareness of how it reads to her parents. Rich descriptions of Georgia's actions and language, recorded in as much detail as possible, gives us raw data to analyse. Adding information about the surrounding context enhances the information. We will become more observant and better at predicting what will help Georgia next in her learning. We can improve our skills further by writing observations as often as we can, taking a number of children, who choose a variety of ways to learn, as subjects. Observations over time can be linked together to show progress or to produce a case study.

Using a case study approach

Gathering observations of Georgia over a period of time can lead to a case study. It tells the story of her early childhood with information about different aspects of her life from different perspectives. The process of writing a case study of Georgia helps us to get to grips with the progress she makes and some of the challenges she faces. From these we can extract the appropriate information. Presenting a case study to colleagues is a brave thing to do – to invite comments and questions and then to rewrite on the basis of these, makes the analysis much stronger.

Georgia is a unique individual and when we observe we are learning how she learns. This is valuable work but remember that it can never be complete.

SUMMARY

- Piaget's Georgia is a 'lone explorer', who constructs knowledge for herself.

- Vygotsky's Georgia is a 'social being', who learns in the context of her family.

- Current theories emphasise Georgia's well-being, involvement and individual approach to learning.

- Georgia's parents are the true experts on Georgia.

- Narrative observations of Georgia provide raw data for analysis and emphasise what Georgia can do.

- Workers and parents can develop a shared vision of the sort of education that they want for Georgia.

We have now been introduced to both the theories underpinning our work with Georgia and her family and to the importance of developing effective observation techniques. In the following chapter we are going to look at how Georgia learns to write and read.

3 GEORGIA LEARNS TO WRITE AND READ

What we make available to the child is a central factor in what the child will and can do.
(Kress, 1995)

In school, literacy teaching and learning is largely overt and specific, whereas at home, it often occurs almost invisibly as an integral part of some everyday activities.
(Weinberger, 1996)

> This chapter describes:
> - Georgia's emergent writing
> - Georgia's emergent reading
> - ideas for supporting literacy development at home, nursery or in reception classes.

From the moment Georgia's parents and Family Worker begin to keep records on her when she is 2 years old, Georgia is motivated to make marks, engage in role play and talk and listen. Her intrinsic motivation and spontaneous desire to engage with writing and reading is sparked off both by the resources available to her and the actions of the people she meets. We can trace the emergence of her writing through examining samples of the marks she makes over a period of time. These marks speak for themselves, offering us a record of Georgia's progress. However, the learning process which will eventually enable Georgia to read and write, begins long before she actually makes marks on paper.

GEORGIA LEARNS TO WRITE

Representation

When Georgia is 2 years 3 months old, 5 minutes after being given a present by her grandmother, she plays handing gifts to everyone at home.

She said 'card', handing a pretend card and 'open it' and 'present', handing each person a bag. Looked very pleased when 'presents' were looked at and commented upon.
(Parent Diary)

Although she does not make marks, she uses 'paper' and a 'bag' to stand for or **represent** a 'card' and 'gift'. She also uses these objects to communicate with each person in turn. There is an emotional response too, indicating the reciprocal nature of the interactions.

At 2 years 5 months, she is with Uncle Paul and plays with 'tickets' and real money, which she carries in a clutch bag. When her grandmother arrives home, she runs to the couch to get a picture for her.

Grandmother: *'She made a mark on it saying "write Mop". She gave me all of the tickets and talked about "paying". She gave me some money and expected me to give her some back.'*

At 2 years 5 months Georgia does some 'writing' for Eloise.

Writing for Eloise

The following month the family are on holiday in Cornwall. One day it rains heavily and Georgia becomes interested in watching the rain and the rabbits in a hutch outside. She does some writing and explains to her mum what her writing says. Then she asks her mum to write down the things that she says out loud.

Writing and drawing

The family visit Georgia's great grandparents and she does a series of pictures for 'Nanny Bonan and Bic' (Nanny Bowman and Vic). She seems to differentiate between drawing and writing and also 'signs' some of her drawings.

At 2 years 7 months Georgia visits her grandmother's house. Her favourite Aunty, Eloise, is still asleep, so Georgia 'writes' her a note.

She explains what she would like to happen.

> **Georgia:** *'Eloise eyes open.'*

Georgia is attempting to communicate her wishes in a written form.

When Georgia is 2 years 8 months, it is her grandmother's birthday. She chooses a card, writes on it and puts it in an envelope. When her dad comes home, Georgia opens it.

> **Mum** (several times): *'It's for Mop's birthday!'*
> **Georgia:** *'Mine. Mine card. Mine birthday.'*

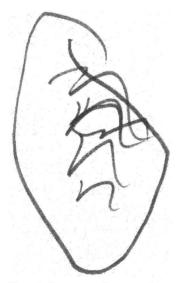

Georgia drew an enclosure and some crosses. She also 'signed' her drawing 'For Nanny Bonan and Bic'

Here Georgia has done some writing next to the enclosure

Cross and enclosure

Georgia's drawing of a Christmas tree, with writing along the bottom

At this stage Georgia seems to enjoy the action of putting the card in an envelope, giving it to someone and getting some acknowledgement for her gift. She does not seem able to wait for her grandmother's birthday.

At 2 years 9 months, Georgia does some drawing and writing that is clearly differentiated. She drew a Christmas tree and wrote her grandmother's name at the bottom.

The following day, Georgia plays 'doctor's' and writes 'prescriptions'. She has a discussion with her mum about surnames.

A couple of weeks later, during a discussion with her grandmother about parties, Georgia remembers that her parents are going to invite the family to their house on Boxing Day. This prompts her to write some invitations.

At 2 years 11 months she does some drawing and writing alongside Jennifer. When Jennifer draws a face, Georgia attempts to draw a face.

When her grandmother stays with the family overnight, Georgia uses one of her grandmother's calligraphy pens to do some 'writing for Kai'. She seems to be intrigued by Kai. She says 'Kai's called the boss'. (Georgia never actually meets Kai but he is her dad's boss.) She also carries a briefcase around and plays at being the boss.

Georgia is now 3 years 2 months.

Mum: '*She accidentally drew an M and yelled at me saying, "Mummy me did Donald's" (meaning McDonald's).*'

Georgia's invitation to her Uncle Paul consists just of her writing

At 3 years 4 months Georgia continues to practise writing curved symbols. Soon after, she copies her mum's writing of 'Harry' and wants to know why 'mum' and 'Colette' (her mum's name) look different. On Father's Day, she asks her mum to write 'daddy' and 'Georgia and Harry' on the card. At 3 years 5 months Georgia writes some 'tickets' and distributes them. At 3 years 6 months she writes a shopping list and pretends to read words from it. Shopping lists or any writing that children see others doing as a routine are, Kress (1995) points out, 'most telling'. He describes them as 'mundane texts'. We have not always recognised the influence of mundane texts in contributing to children's literacy development.

When Georgia and her family are on holiday, she has a turn on a scooter and although it is only early August, she writes a letter to Santa Claus to ask for a scooter.

Here Georgia says she is writing her own name and her grandmother's name.

Georgia wrote her own name

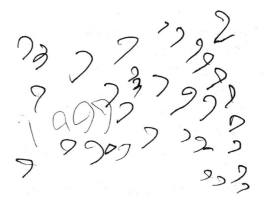

This is Georgia's grandmother's name

By now Georgia is very aware that her parents (and sometimes her grandparents) write down what she says and does. At 3 years 6 months after playing with a difficult spherical puzzle at her grandparents' house, she asks her grandmother 'to write down that I can do that game'. Georgia is intentionally recording information as she sees others doing. This is an example of Georgia beginning to understand the communication that happens in her particular 'social context' (Pollard, 1996).

Georgia is excited when she receives a postcard from Aunty Eloise, who is away on holiday. She seems to be becoming aware of the forms of some conventional symbols. She does 'loads of kisses' on a get well card for her dad, but tells him '. . . me did one wrong'. At 3 years 7 months Georgia begins to recognise and to represent letters that are significant to her.

> **Mum:** *'She did some drawing outside and talked about G for Georgia and H for Harry. (She could write H but not G.)'*

At 3 years 8 months, Georgia uses her grandparents' computer to do 'writing'.

'G's and 'H's crop up in Georgia's drawings

Grandmother: *'She wanted to do my name and Georgia – talked about G for Georgia, H for Harry and mummy's number.'*

It does not seem a coincidence that while Georgia is struggling to write the letter G, she seeks out and participates in other activities which involve circular movements and enclosures (Athey, 1990). The following extracts from Georgia's parents' diary illustrate this point.

Georgia spends a lot of time making friendship bracelets to fit various people. She is deeply involved and when her dad says 'Men don't wear them', she offers, 'Want me to make you a really nice one you don't put on?' and 'Dad, want some to hang down your glasses?' (at 3 years 7 months)

Georgia has been trying to tie shoe laces. (at 3 years 7 months)

Came home today with some embroidery thread and asked me to tie it around her wrist. (at 3 years 7 months)

Has been playing 'Ring-a-roses' and 'Farmer's in the Den'. (at 3 years 7 months and 3 years 8 months)

Asks me to put her broken watch on for her. (at 3 years 8 months)

Says she is going 'to tie something around her waist'. (at 3 years 8 months)

Georgia begins going to nursery, where her early interests are stories, using the computer and building. At 3 years 8 months, Georgia seems interested in using up all of the maple blocks. She spends time placing them individually, which later may help her to understand that individual letters make words.
   Gura (1992 (ed)) describes

The kinds of knowledge the child will discover about the physical qualities of unit blocks . . . Blocks occupy spaces that correspond to their shape, form, length, width and volume . . . Blocks can be arranged and rearranged.

Individual blocks have the potential to be manipulated and placed in various ways, for example, 'next to', 'on top of', 'under'. In her early writing Georgia represents whole lines or vertical lists rather than individual letters. In a similar way, Gura points out that 'a brick in a wall is not necessarily understood as part of a whole by the young child'. Georgia, by manipulating each block, may be

Georgia uses individual blocks to create a complex whole – this may help her to understand how letters make words and words make sentences

beginning to understand each block as part of her whole building. This is similar to understanding that individual letters make up words and that words make up sentences or passages of text.

When Georgia is 3 years 8 months, she seems to understand that individual letters make up words. When Georgia is writing on her grandmother's birthday card, her mum spells out 'M o p' and describes how to write the letters – 'M for McDonalds', 'a round shape' and 'a round shape with a line'.

Four days later, Georgia writes her dad's name, 'Ian' in the parent diary.

A couple of months later, when Georgia is 3 years 11 months, she writes her own name conventionally for the first time. Two days later she 'verbally spelt GEORGIA and IAN'. She practises writing her name, frequently incorporating

Georgia writes Mop, addressing her grandmother's birthday card

the letters into her drawings. She is very keen to draw a recognisable Christmas tree. After constructing and manipulating a plastic marble run which she is given for Christmas, Georgia manages to draw zig-zags. She makes several attempts before she is satisfied with the form of her tree.

Drawing a tree like this is a complex representation, which involves making a zig-zag (Athey, 1990) into an enclosure, while retaining the zig-zag edge. The Christmas tree is Georgia's co-ordination of zig-zags, previously used to represent writing, and enclosures, previously used for friendship bracelets, round letters and drawings.

Learning about words

At nursery when Georgia is 4 years old, she and Angela, her current Family Worker, look at a book that has been brailled.

> **Angela:** *'Georgia's query was why was the braille not the same size (length) as the print?'*

When Georgia is 4 years 1 month, she writes that she wants to visit Thomas the Tank Engine.

Georgia makes several attempts to draw a Christmas tree before she is happy with the result

Georgia can write her own name and 'Thomas' for Thomas the Tank Engine

Georgia is progressing fast. Two weeks after writing about Thomas the Tank Engine, it is her grandad's birthday. She writes her own name and her brother's as well as her grandad's and lots of kisses.

At 4 years 2 months Georgia's concern seems to be the length of each word she writes and the space it occupies. Georgia's mum notes that she is 'writing and fitting words into a space'. Georgia has a discussion with her grandmother who is pointing to words as she reads. Georgia seems surprised.

Georgia addresses an envelope

Georgia: *'Does that say me?'*
Grandmother: *'Yes'.*
Georgia: *'Just M and E?'*
Gran: *'Yes.'*
Georgia: *'Just two letters?'*
Gran: *'Yes'.*

Mum: *'Later on when she was writing names she wrote Georgia quite small "so it'll fit".'*

Lee and Das Gupta (1995), in a discussion about young children learning to read, say that,

Even very obvious features of words, spoken or written length, for example, may be difficult for children to perceive.

Georgia uses a narrow strip of paper and writes a list of names that will fit

Georgia is sensitive to word length at this time and naturally learns which names are short and which are longer. This will contribute to her general understanding when she learns to write and read more formally.

At 4 years 4 months, Georgia writes her full name.

Five months after Georgia writes her name conventionally for the first time, she is able to write her full name

At nursery Georgia frequently paints. Labelling her work with her name is important to her and seems to be part of the creative process. Georgia announces that she is 'going to do another one and another one and another one until the paper's all finished.'

Georgia leaves nursery in July. In September she starts school and her favourite Aunty Eloise goes to University. Over the first few months Georgia is strongly motivated to draw pictures and to write to Eloise. Eloise always replies and this encourages Georgia to continue to communicate with her by post. One of her first sentences of writing is 'I love Eloise'. There is obviously an emotional dimension to Georgia's desire to communicate with Eloise, to whom she has been closely 'attached' from birth. Meek (1982) says that 'Reading, writing, thinking, knowing and feeling are all bound up in each other'.

Looking back with Georgia's parents

Georgia's parents acknowledge her early attempts at making marks as important and this undoubtedly encourages her to continue to make marks. Often the marks are made in the context of role play.

> **Dad:** *'There was always role play because of the older children. They used to play buses and they would use tickets.'*

It seems that from when Georgia is about a year old, the older children would include her in some of their games. As she becomes older herself (about 2 years of age), she begins to initiate role play, either alone or with others.

> **Mum:** *'Her role play was about work, school or families. I remember her playing "sisters". She used to play shops or Doctors.'*

Georgia (at 7 years) remembers playing 'sisters' at nursery.

> **Georgia:** *'Stephanie was the mum 'cos she liked it – we would get the dolls from nursery and I would pretend to be five or something and help her.'*

Her dad remembers that there was a sort of pecking order.

> **Dad:** *'Stephanie was in charge – she was the eldest, then Georgia, then Laura.'*

Using role play
On one occasion, at home, Georgia plays alone at being Kai, her dad's boss, who she has heard about but never actually met. Her mum thinks Kai intrigues

Georgia partly because she does not meet him. He seems a powerful person. Kai can tell her dad what to do.

> **Mum:** *'She seemed to be working out what Kai did, without seeing him for herself.'*

Being Kai involves Georgia in transporting things (papers and briefcase), and in writing, both of which she enjoys. When Georgia becomes a fluent writer she continues to finds ways to practise.

> **Dad:** *'She would plan parties months ahead in order to write lists of names.'*
> **Mum:** *'She always liked lists and names. Even now, she does lists for her party, what she wants for Christmas etc. She looks through the Next Directory, ticks what she likes and makes a list of page number, item, description, price etc. – sometimes asterisks things she really wants.'*

During our discussion this is borne out by Georgia who produces a chart on the spot.

georgia	cath	georgia	cath
things I liked at nursery.	Things I wrote.	things I like now	Things I wrote
Dressing up. Playing with the blocks. Playing mums and babies. Playing in the home corner. Playing with water. Playing in wood work area. Playing in sand. Playing on the horse.		Reading Secret Seven books Goosebumps and The Mystery of.... Writing stories. Playing clapping games and singing songs to it. ✳ listening to music.	

Georgia has always had writing materials available to her at home. By the time she is 2 years old, her parents place a low coffee table in one corner of the living-room. On this table are Georgia's things, felt pens, scissors, paper and real money.

Exploring Georgia's motivation to write

In Chapter One, Georgia's mum describes her as a 'people person' and this seems to be the key to understanding her motivation to write. Whitehead (1997) talks about 'the inspiration for early writing'.

> *The inspiration for writing arises partly from children's perceptions of it as a high status activity – something that is done by significant people in their social world.*

Georgia's early experience of

- playing with older children, who are already writers

- visiting her parents' workplaces

- attending a nursery, where records and documentation are part of the daily work of the adults

- being aware that close adults write down what she does and says

all appear to contribute to her place in a world of writers. It is not surprising that, within this context, Georgia makes meaningful marks fairly early.

The emergent nature of writing development has been widely studied (Weinberger, 1996; Whitehead, 1997). Weinberger says that,

> *Even in the early stages, children's writing often takes on visual similarities with the script the child is most familiar with.*

Georgia, like most young writers, has a sense of the joined up nature of writing and this is how she first represents the marks she sees adults and older children make.

Writing one's own name

The motivation to learn to write one's own name is common to many children. Whitehead attributes more meaning to the writing of one's own name than merely making the right marks.

Personal names are charged with meaning: they encapsulate our sense of self-worth and our place in the world.

It certainly seems important to Georgia, as an emergent writer, to be able to write the letters of her name and to place them in the right order.

Understanding what the marks mean

The marks young children make have been widely studied, but there have been fewer studies of meaning and communication in relation to emergent writing. Some followers of Vygotsky (Moll, 1990; Goodman and Goodman, 1990; Blanck, 1990) believe that children learn language as a complex whole within a social context. Goodman and Goodman say:

> *The whole-language view of literacy development is thus an immersion view. Children growing up in literate societies are surrounded by print. They begin to be aware of the functions of written language and to play at its use long before they come to school.*

This view seems to fit how Georgia spontaneously uses the print and writing practices she comes across and makes them her own, constantly setting herself new challenges. In most cases, from 2 to 5 years Georgia is:

- acting out what she has seen

- imitating the sorts of writing activities she has seen

- communicating something real.

Whole body movement and manipulation of materials

There are other actions that Georgia is intrinsically motivated to try out, repeatedly and in different ways. Her sustained interest in enclosures when she is struggling to write the letter 'G' is a good example. The evidence indicates that the actual mark (the 'G') is like the tip of an iceberg. The greater part, which is hidden, is all of the related actions, some that involve whole body movement and others that involve the manipulation of materials. It is not a coincidence that while Georgia is making enclosures she becomes sensitive to and able to use related language, for example 'tie around'. Evidence from the Froebel Project (Athey, 1990) supports the idea that 'speech is acquired in synchrony with acquired meanings'. In other words, children learn to use appropriate language at the same time as they gain concepts.

Georgia's 'writing related' activities precede her 'reading related' activities, but only slightly. The records indicate clusters of activity, for example, the records show a month of listening and talking, followed by two weeks of writing. It is as though certain activities come to the fore for a matter of weeks.

GEORGIA LEARNS TO READ

Stories feature strongly in Georgia's life. She has favourite books, which are stories or rhymes, and also favourite tales about real events. However, she begins 'reading' by imitating the actions of others.

The first record that indicates Georgia's understanding of meaning conveyed by print, is at 2 years 6 months.

> **Mum:** *'Georgia wanted another fromage frais. I said "What flavour was that one?" She went over, picked it up, turned it around and looked closely at each side of the container and then said "30p"!'*

✳ Rueda (1990) says,

> *Clay (1975) and Read (1975) have shown that children know a lot about literacy before they can write and read in an 'adult' conventional sense.*

Often Georgia wants to listen to stories over and over again. When she is 2 years 7 months, something unusual happens, and she is keen to be the 'teller' rather than the 'told'.

> **Grandmother:** *'When they came in today, Georgia was desperate to tell me they had seen a bike lying on the ground. Her mum thought she had seen a person lying beside it, so they went back to have a look. They thought it might have been a car crash. The person seemed to be drunk and got up and rode off on the bike.'*

Georgia is able to tell this story to her grandmother in the right sequence. To relate a story in the order of what happens is very skilled. Georgia relates her very recent firsthand experience, which she has been discussing with her mum. Two things are important. Firstly, the significance of what she has observed has made her 'excited': the neurons in her brain are literally 'firing' away (Carter, 1998) and increasing the intensity of her perception of the dramatic events. Secondly, Georgia may have already developed a 'script' from past experiences which helps her to categorise this new experience (Gardner, 1991).

Katherine Nelson has named this area 'the use of scripts.'

. . . a script entails the identification and ordering of those features that are reliably associated with a recurrent event.

These scripts serve as an entry point to storytelling and story understanding.

We heard at the beginning of this section that Georgia has listened to stories from books and also stories about real events in the family. The stories she has heard provide 'sequences of events against which newly encountered events are judged'.

At 2 years 9 months Georgia makes connections between written words and songs and also adds her own communication.

Grandmother: *'Georgia sang me some Christmas carols when we were trying to get Harry to sleep. She brought over a book, went through it and knew which carol was on each page. Suddenly she started singing Baa Baa Black Sheep. She went and fetched her nursery rhyme book and started singing rhymes. (Again as though she was reading them.) She began adding 'at the hotel' at the end of each rhyme. I said, "Where did the hotel come from?" She said "At the wedding." ' (The family were going to a wedding and would be staying overnight in a hotel.)*

It is months later, when Georgia is 3 years 2 months, that she demonstrates her recognition of a conventional symbol when she accidentally drew an M and says, 'Mummy me did Donald's' (meaning McDonalds). Here Georgia links **encoding** (writing using conventional symbols) with **decoding** (reading from conventional symbols).

On the same day, Georgia remarks that a lorry without writing on the side is 'not Safeway lorry'. Later that day, Georgia's mum got out some new books for her. She immediately recognised one of a series and said 'An Alfie book!' (referring to the series of books by Shirley Hughes).

At 3 years 4 months, Georgia is making comparisons between words when she asked why 'mum' looked different to 'Colette'.

Although, at this stage, Georgia is beginning to recognise conventional symbols and to understand that there is a code to crack, she still does pretend writing and pretends to read from her lists. The transition between pretend reading and real reading is interesting. Georgia does not reject her pretend reading just because she now begins to understand that a set of symbols represent sounds (Riley, 1995). The two stages seem to overlap.

When Georgia starts attending nursery, she begins to 'sign' her work with her name. This is a usual convention for the adults at nursery and therefore has a real world value for Georgia.

Reaching a plateau

For about 4 months, there does not appear to be any progress as far as reading is concerned, Georgia does, however, listen to lots of stories both at home and at nursery, during this period.

When Georgia is 4 years old she is interested in braille and asks 'does it say the same as that?' pointing at the print.

A few days later, Georgia picks up a card from the floor of her grandmother's car, as they are driving along.

Grandmother: *'It's from one of the shops.'*
Georgia: *'It might be from Aldi [pause] it's from Asda, I think, it says A S D A.'*

For about 3 months after her fourth birthday, Georgia frequently asks which letters words begin with.

At nursery when Georgia is 4 years, she listens to familiar stories and when her Family Worker is reading, Georgia completes sentences correctly, indicating that she has learnt parts of stories off by heart.

At home when Georgia is 4 years 3 months, she pretends to read a story and includes Harry as part of the storyline.

Mum: *'Georgia held the book entitled* My Naughty Little Sister at the Fair. *She pretended to read, making up a story which included Harry.'*

A week later, she is less willing to include him. Georgia was reading her school leaflet out loud – Harry sat next to her.

Georgia: *'It's not a story.'*
Dad: *'He just wants to sit next to you.'*
Georgia: *'I'll just read it in my head then, so he can't hear it.'* (This indicates an understanding of silent reading, as well as a desire to keep information about school to herself.)

Mum: *'Georgia still asks me to read her school information pack for her bedtime story. She knows lines of it by heart – referring to the school uniform. She also talks about what colour uniform she wants and what drink she will take in her packed lunch, as "fizzy drinks are unsuitable"! (Georgia repeats the whole phrase from the leaflet.)'*

Looking back with Georgia's parents

Both parents remember that Georgia 'was always interested in books'.

> **Mum:** *'She always liked books over and over again.'*
> **Dad:** *'Amy and Jennifer used to read to her.'*

Her mum remembers that her favourite stories were *The Tiger Who Came to Tea*, *Papa, Please Get Me the Moon* and a *Christmas Carol Book*. She knew the carol book off by heart and 'you couldn't miss one out 'cos she would know'.

Learning about real life
Georgia likes to know about real life.

> **Mum:** *'She used to love my pregnancy books when I was expecting Harry. I think she liked anything that related to anything real.'*

Before she was born, her parents were involved in a serious car accident. Her dad remembers that she wanted to hear about the car crash.

> **Dad:** *'We used to tell her over and over and over again.'*

Georgia may be using this 'script' to retell what happens when she and her mum see someone lying on the ground and possibly injured (Gardner, 1991).

Learning through books
Books are Georgia's favourite medium.

> **Mum:** *'She wasn't bothered about watching videos or telly or anything.'*

Georgia (at 7 years) remembers a story.

> **Georgia:** *'Avocado Baby was about a really strong baby who pushes the car.'*

> **Mum:** *'The school leaflet was her bedtime story for about a month.'*

Georgia seems to have knowledge of a range of stories and, at nursery, could choose either familiar stories or new ones.

Exploring Georgia's motivation to read

Georgia may have seen reading, as well as writing, as a 'high status activity' (Whitehead, 1997). She is surrounded by people who can read and she is aware of the exciting content of many stories. Georgia is eager to gain information, particularly about real events in her world. Her need to hear stories over and over and over again indicates her sheer pleasure in this activity.

Although, for the purposes of this book, I have separated the accounts of writing and reading, they are, of course, tied very closely together. Riley (1995) describes 'developing literary competence':

> Concepts about print are slowly acquired through the emergent literacy phase; they develop through rich and meaningful encounters with print in the twin processes of early reading and primitive message writing.

When Georgia begins to learn 'the sounds that letters make' (Lee and Das Gupta, 1995), for example how to spell and recognise ASDA, she is aware of her own progress. Simultaneously, she makes progress in her use of language, and again, seems to be aware of her own advances. Georgia often self-corrects and comments on her own correct use of language, for example, at 3 years 6 months she says, 'Me say that right – Laura at our house yesterday'. She is referring, not only to her correct use of language, but to the concept of 'yesterday', which she uses correctly in this instance.

Georgia learns about reading

Georgia's parents acknowledge her early pretend reading and are also prepared to respond to her queries about sounds and letters. This way of responding in a 'casual rather than didactic way' (Weinberger, 1996) to her queries may be significant. Weinberger describes this way of responding as characteristic of fostering literacy development.

Amy and Jennifer read to Georgia, which may give her a sense of her own future as a reader. She learns the content of the stories they read to her, as well as learning that reading is pleasurable.

The ease with which Georgia is able to choose stories at nursery is also significant and may be the result of her earlier experiences at home. In her longitudinal study, Weinberger (1996) found that,

> Children's familiarity and enjoyment of books at home probably made the children more likely to choose to look at books on their own when they came to nursery.

So, Georgia starts nursery and, subsequently, school with the general idea that books are enjoyable and informative, and also feeling confident about extending her range of knowledge through books.

IDEAS FOR SUPPORTING LITERACY DEVELOPMENT

Although Georgia's story is presented in chronological order, we know that she does not learn in a simple, linear way. As adults, we need to be open to any opportunities for learning and teaching, as they present themselves. We can draw from this record of Georgia's emergent writing and reading some **principles** and **strategies** that we might apply to other children learning to write and read. Principles are our firm beliefs that underpin what we do. Strategies are the ways through which we stand by our principles.

Principles in developing Georgia's literacy

1   Start by making close observations of Georgia.
2   Provide open ended materials for making marks and role play.
3   Assess what Georgia knows.
4   Extend from what Georgia knows and wants to know.

Start by making close observations
All children in the UK have some experiences of literacy. It is up to the adults in Georgia's life to discover what she has noticed in her environment. We can do this by watching her at play, by listening to her parents and by responding to her questions. It is important to treat Georgia as an individual. When we respond to her as an individual we increase her pleasure, competence and self-esteem (Roberts, 1995). We can respond immediately in a variety of ways, from giving her our undivided attention for a couple of seconds to introducing a story we think she will like.

Provide materials
Georgia needs a range of open-ended materials with which to make marks. The quality of materials provided does make a difference. Georgia was interested in improving the form of what she drew and wrote. Felt pens produce much better marks for beginners than thin crayons. I would argue for quality and range: chalk, pens, pencils, sticks, cotton buds, paint brushes, rollers, knives and so on. Offering a wide range opens up the possibilities for Georgia. Cloaks, hats and shoes often attract her, enticing her to get into role and to reveal what she is thinking about.

Assess what Georgia knows

The best time to assess what Georgia knows is when she is 'deeply involved' (Laevers, 1997) and using materials spontaneously. Laevers (1993) has shown that, when a learner is 'deeply involved', 'the mind is exactly doing what is favourable to its own development'. (The involvement signals are listed in Chapter Two.) If we provide an environment, rich in the type of materials described and with adults who are interested in discovering her world, Georgia will provide the starting points for discussion through her actions. We must discuss what she is learning with parents and colleagues. Georgia revealed her understanding of writing and communication through writing materials to adults who were prepared to encourage and support her. Telling stories and writing alongside Georgia contributed to her knowledge and helped us to assess what she knew at any one point in time.

Extend from what Georgia knows and wants to know

When Georgia asks questions, usually it is because she genuinely wants to know something. Therefore, her questions provide a guide to what she is ready to learn. Georgia often asks her parents questions. Nursery practitioners may also be asked. When Georgia wanted to know which letters words begin with, she was actively seeking out the knowledge she was ready to learn. Her parents and workers could simply tell her what she asked each time or tell her in different ways: by singing songs which include letter sounds, by having an alphabet frieze for her to look at or by playing games which include sounds. Providing these different routes, with no pressure to take up the knowledge in any particular way, preserves Georgia's enjoyment of learning.

Strategies for helping Georgia to develop her literacy

1   Practitioners from nursery or school can visit Georgia and her family at home, discuss writing and reading and try to discover what her parents think about literacy.

2   Good reading material should be available and accessible to Georgia, giving her time to look at books and to make her own marks, with and without an adult present. Set up a lending library and encourage Georgia to bring in her favourite books or videos from home.

3   Extend Georgia's interests through the 'form' or repeated pattern of behaviour (for example, enclosure) as well as through 'content' (Athey, 1990), (eg the bracelet).

4   Encourage Georgia to talk to adults and to other children. Have toy mobile phones available, puppets, role play areas and small world equipment.

5   Capitalise on any special events or on what Georgia plays spontaneously, for example in the home corner or outside.

6   Do some research on current trends – what is currently on TV for this age group? What is the latest toy or street or playground game being played by the older children Georgia knows?

Visit Georgia at home and discuss literacy

We know that children who are familiar with books, choose books more readily and may extend their knowledge through reading. If we begin by validating the literacy that exists in Georgia's home environment, not by judging her home as better than another but by seeing families as different to each other, we can discover a starting point for Georgia at nursery. Although Georgia did not choose to learn through watching videos, some children access stories through watching videos and learning a favourite script off by heart. We can make links with home by what we provide at nursery or school. I am not suggesting that children at school or nursery watch videos as part of the curriculum, but we can provide props that encourage Georgia and other children to act out stories and we may be able to provide the original story on which a favourite video is based.

We can also ensure that the nursery environment includes similar writing and reading materials to those Georgia would see at home: junk mail, yellow pages, a catalogue, payment card or airmail letters in another language. Whatever is familiar is a starting point.

Have good reading material available

If we want Georgia to learn to read and to feel confident with books, we must offer her a range of books. Books need to be chosen carefully to ensure that they are not racist, sexist, disablist or tokenist. We also need to consider the cultural messages that we are passing on to Georgia through literature. Reference books are important and are often more popular with boys. Georgia cannot learn to use and take care of books if they are out of her reach. We can display books on low shelves and encourage Georgia to help herself to books whenever she wants to.

Writing and reading materials can be offered to Georgia in various areas of the nursery. For example, notebooks, writing paper and envelopes can be placed in the home corner, and chalk, clipboards and pencils can be used outside.

Setting up a system to lend books to Georgia and other children means that all families can have access to materials at home. Encouraging Georgia to bring her favourite books or videos from home means that we can have access to her family's materials.

Making books using Georgia's role play or the stories she invents as the text enables Georgia to become the author. Graves (1983) describes a wonderful project in which schoolchildren write and review books for each other, making a classroom library of their own works.

Extend what we offer

We have seen how writing and reading are only the tip of the iceberg. Athey (1990) shows how we can extend Georgia's thinking by closely observing her repeated actions and offering content to 'feed' those patterns or repeated actions. We might suppose that, when Georgia was repeatedly drawing curves and enclosures, we could only extend through offering writing materials and paper. But she was exploring something bigger: going around and enclosure. There are all sorts of materials, games and stories we could offer to help her get to grips with going around.

We noticed that Georgia was sensitive to related language when she was forming concepts. Nutbrown (1994) links the content of various stories with the 'forms' or 'schemas' that children explore. For example, when Georgia is interested in enveloping, Nutbrown suggests that she might enjoy *A Dark, Dark Tale* by Ruth Brown (1992), in which successive coverings are removed to reveal a mouse asleep inside a box.

Encourage Georgia to talk

Narrative begins with the telling of tales (Whitehead, 1997). Talking, therefore, precedes writing and reading. Some children will only explore talk using a phone or puppets. Providing the right props will encourage Georgia to talk, act and improve her organisational skills necessary for later writing and reading. Listening to Georgia conveys the message that what she is saying is as important as what adults say.

Capitalise on special events and spontaneous play

We can discover what Georgia is thinking by closely observing her spontaneous play. We can add literacy content to almost any game. We can provide anything from a shopping list to a memo from the boss to genuine instructions for constructing a new piece of equipment. We can allow Georgia to be involved in real writing or reading. Having systems such as registers or records of whose turn it is to take part in particular activities, such as cooking or going on the computer, is a real reason to read and write daily.

Special events such as birthdays, Christmas and Diwali all have the potential for literacy related activities. Writing invitations, decorating cakes and writing place cards can be part of these events. Georgia loves authenticity and will know when she is doing a genuine job. We need to give Georgia enough time to do these real jobs and be prepared to finish off for her if the task proves too difficult.

Do some research

Anything older children do Georgia perceives as a 'high status activity' (Whitehead, 1997). These activities are, therefore, worthy of our attention. When the 'dispositions' to learn are strong, Georgia will make 'decisions' about getting involved and about taking responsibility for her own learning as far as she can (Carr et al, 1998). So whether the latest craze is a cult toy or TV programme, it is worth finding out what is in it as far as literacy development is concerned.

SUMMARY

- Georgia learns to write through imitating writers, recognising print in the environment, recognising significant words and practising movements in various ways with a range of materials.

- Georgia learns to read through listening to stories, imitating readers, recognising environmental print and asking questions about sounds and letters.

- There are many principles and strategies for supporting Georgia's literacy development.

We have now looked at how Georgia approached writing and reading and at how her parents and nursery workers supported her emergent literacy. In the next chapter we will be looking at how Georgia's understanding of Maths develops.

4 UNDERSTANDING MATHEMATICAL CONCEPTS

Mathematics – the abstract science of number, quantity and space studied in its own right.
(Tulloch (Ed), 1990)

Certainty is a word that mathematicians often use when they try to describe the appeal of what they do.
(Hoffman, 1998)

The kind of certainty that Hoffman is talking about involves proving that something is always the same.

> The mathematical concepts that Georgia spends most time exploring from 2 to 5 years are:
>
> - quantity, including counting and dividing
>
> - size and fit
>
> - time, particularly chronology.

Long before Georgia's parents realise that she is exploring mathematical ideas, Georgia spends a lot of her time carrying objects about. Often she gives objects to people, only to take them back from them seconds later and then carry them about some more. She is transporting. While she is doing this, she is proving to herself that although her load looks different depending on whether it is held by five different people, or whether she carries it in a bag or pushes it in a trolley, it is never-the-less exactly the same load. It only changes if another object is added or something is removed.

- As a 1-year-old, she pushes her trolley about – sometimes with wooden bricks in it and sometimes with other objects.

- As a 2-year-old, she pushes her buggy, rides her truck, and carries various bags, purses and buckets. She carries objects in these different containers distributing them and gathering them together over and over again.

This strong transporting behaviour contributes to Georgia's mathematical future (Athey, 1990). Georgia will eventually understand that the number of objects stays the same (or is **invariant**) unless anything is added or taken away (Lee and Das Gupta, 1995).

We observed what Georgia knew about writing from the marks she made and what she knew about reading from what she said. Mathematical and scientific understanding involves abstract concepts. Therefore, in this chapter and the next, we can only speculate about what Georgia might be learning. These speculations usually take the form of questions following direct observations of her actions.

EXPLORING IDEAS ABOUT QUANTITY AND AMOUNT

Georgia plays with real money and often this is what she manipulates, carries about and distributes. Before she understands conventional counting, at 2 years 5 months she has a sense of what happens when money changes hands.

> **Mum:** *'She took a couple of coins out of a tin and was talking to herself, saying "20, 20". Then she gave me some coins and said "Play moneypops".'*

A few days later, Georgia is playing with tickets and money.

> **Mum:** *'She gave me all of the tickets and talked about paying. She gave me some money and waited for me to give her some back ... She shared the money out giving me all of the copper coins and she kept the silver ones. She referred to the 20p as a "choo choo" ie a ride on a toy train at the supermarket.'*

Georgia seems to be drawing on her experiences of going to the supermarket and paying for goods as well as paying for rides. The tickets may connect with her frequent visits to Wicksteed Park as she often says 'Pay the man' when manipulating tickets and money. She seems to understand that 20p pays for a ride. This is an example of something from the everyday context of her own life which Georgia quickly learns and uses in her play.

Nunes et al (1993) describe 'street mathematics' learnt by children and adults, who have had no schooling but who experience 'everyday practices'. Vygotsky would say that Georgia is learning 'everyday concepts' about money through her experiences (Moll, 1990).

Using language to describe quantity

Four months later, when Georgia is 2 years 9 months, she demonstrates her ideas about quantity in the language she uses. She talks about running 'really, really, giant fast' to describe great speed.

A few days later, Georgia is playing with money.

> *'Had money in purse, inside box. Talked to herself about 'paying sixty', said 'don't know if I've got sixty.'*
> (Parent Diary)

'Sixty' seems to be a number she likes the sound of. It is not unusual for children to have favourite numbers or words. (Carruthers, 1997)

Georgia at 2 years 9 months continues to try out language which relates to the concept of greater amount or quantity.

> *Giant . . . signifies greatest amount e.g. <u>giant</u> quiet if you want her to be <u>very</u> quiet.*
> (Parent Diary)

She is more specific when she says, 'Daddy been London on six times.'

Georgia tries out a different word to describe amount.

> *'Father' signifies 'very' or greatest amount of something.*
> (Parent Diary)

It is several months later, on her brother's first birthday, when Georgia is 3 years 3 months that she, again, reveals her knowledge of quantity.

> *When everyone but the family had left, Georgia got out some cards with numbers on and played a game for about an hour with Mop, Pop, Uncle Paul, Mum and Dad. She was definitely in charge 'sharing' and telling Paul and Pop 'You only allowed three'. Also 'I need number one 'cos Harry's one'. Several times during the game she said she had 'winned' or someone else or two others had 'winned'. She asked me how old I was. Also said 'I need number four 'cos I gonna be four next year'. Several times she said some of the players were 'in' and some were 'out'. She recognised numbers (1, 2, 3, 4 and 5) and at times said to Paul or Pop, 'You got number five?' or 'You got number three?' If they had and they showed her, she would swap it, usually for a lower number or tell them they were 'allowed' less cards than they had. Mostly she had more cards than anyone else.*
> (Parent Diary)

Clearly Georgia has some experience of older children or adults playing cards. She is imitating or replicating, to some extent, what she has seen or been part of. If she has been part of a game, the rules seemed arbitrary to her. However, in her representation of a card game, Georgia does show that she has a good grasp of the order of numbers, at least from one to five and the values associated with those numbers. There also seems to be a gender aspect, in that she appears to identify with the other females and to pick on Pop and Paul as though they are from an opposing team. (This is implicit rather than explicit. The hidden message seems to be that whatever hand the males are dealt, they will not win as Georgia regularly reviews what they are holding and swaps it for something less or lower.) She may be identifying with the women rather than the men and possibly seeing herself as part of a larger group.

Two months later, when Georgia is 3 years 5 months, she plays dropping a tennis ball and catching it, counting up to 12 catches. (Now she can keep in mind the quantity without being able to see the objects that make up that quantity.)

Georgia continues to play with money, sometimes lining it up and counting it. She also cuts paper 'into tiny bits for Eloise for money for the till'. Georgia may be puzzling over whether it is the same amount of paper when cut up into tiny pieces.

Dividing and connecting materials

On holiday, at 3 years 6 months, Georgia cuts up mushrooms and cucumber for the salad – as she gets towards the end of the job, she cuts them smaller and smaller. Is it a sign that she is enjoying cutting so much that she wants to prolong the time spent on this job? Does she wonder whether the vegetables increase in amount when cut up? This links closely with something Georgia does early in the morning, at home, when she is 3 years 7 months.

> *This morning Georgia came to me in bed and told me she had some blu-tack and that she was going to do a picture and put it up. A bit later, she asked me to come and see 'cos it looks really good'. She had cut up pictures from a travel brochure into quite small pieces and then blu-tacked them to my bathroom wall.*
> (Parent Diary)

Georgia is able to view what she has divided like pieces of a jigsaw laid out on the floor. Is she looking to see whether the parts can be put back together to form a whole picture? Piaget (1951) offers an example of a child 'breaking up' clay and putting it together again.

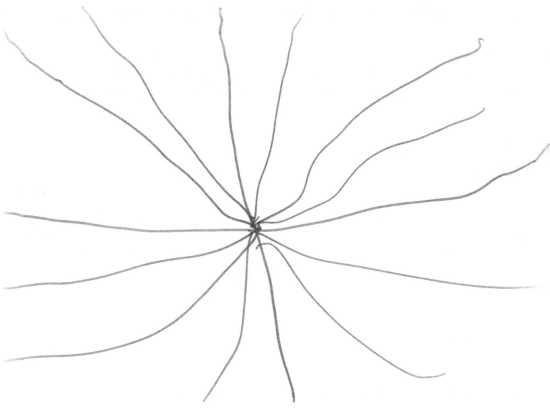

Georgia experiments with dividing space

Around the same time, Georgia's interest in division is reflected in her language and in her drawing.

> *Georgia tells her dad she has been a little bit naughty and a little bit good.*
> (Parent Diary)

This is like dividing her day into different parts.

Athey (1990) found that some children in the Froebel project *'divided circles into two halves for various representations'*.

At nursery, at 3 years 5 months, Georgia builds using maple unit blocks. The blocks are mathematically related to one another and this is important to Georgia when she is learning about division and parts of a whole. Gura (1992) says that children have 'an intuitive urge to unite' parts of dissected wholes.

At the same age, when Georgia uses the computer at nursery, she demands five copies of her picture. She explains why to Alison, her Family Worker.

Georgia: *'One for mummy, one for daddy, one for Harry, one for me, one for you (Alison).'*

Close people are her first references when deciding 'how many'. Georgia is *multiplying* her one picture by five in order to *share* it between all of her important people.

An understanding of counting

At 3 years 9 months, Georgia seems to be on the cusp of understanding counting. She can count in a conventional, stable order and knows about making each number correspond with one object being counted. She also knows that the final number is the total amount. Gelman and Gallistel (1978) call these 'how to count' principles. However, at home, Georgia sets herself a difficult counting task.

> *Georgia is playing with eight 2p coins, whilst looking out of the window.*
> **Georgia:** *'I'm going to make a circle.'*
> (Parent Diary)

Is she representing the formation of the houses in the close?

> **Georgia:** *'I'm going to count them now.'*
> *Georgia then counted from one of the coins near the top – and counted nine – she didn't remember where she started!*
> (Parent Diary)

It is much more tricky to count a circle of objects than a line of objects. Georgia has been arranging money in lines for a long time and is trying out a different arrangement.

Ten days later, again at home, Georgia demonstrates her understanding of what a total of three means.

> *Georgia has been doing different '3s' eg holding up her thumb and first two fingers, then just her first three fingers, then her last three fingers – she seems to be getting the idea of the amount rather than 'naming' each item with a number.*
> (Parent Diary)

Georgia continues practising counting and when she is 4 years 2 months she counts to about 60. Georgia also continues to work on division and parts of whole objects. At nursery, at 3 years 9 months, Georgia plays with dough.

Rolling the dough backwards and forwards, now adding little pieces from the table and rolling them into the larger piece.
(Observation by Family Worker)

Dividing and combining dough is very different because the shape of the whole lump can change. Is it the same when it is a long sausage as it is when it is a round flat shape?

Georgia continues to fold and cut paper both at nursery and at home.

Estimating and counting on

At 3 years 10 months, when she is about to travel to London by train, Georgia estimates that there will be ten tunnels between Kettering and London. She spends the journey counting them. Georgia is able to 'keep the meaning of the problem in mind' (Nunes, 1995). She remembers her estimate and 'counts on' as the train goes through each tunnel (McLellan, 1997).

Understanding the limits

Then at 3 years 11 months, Georgia becomes interested in limits (or what is *finite* and what is *infinite*). She has already experimented with using up all of the maple blocks at nursery. She is using the computer at her grandparents' house and suddenly asks, 'Will the G's run out?' Her grandmother explains what can limit the computer's use and about the printer using up ink.

Months later, at nursery, when she is painting, Georgia (aged 4 years 5 months) says she is going to do 'another one and another one and another one until the paper is all gone'. This may be to prolong enjoyment or to test out whether she is allowed to use up all of the resources on the table.

Georgia shows a well-developed understanding of the use of fuel, when, at 4 years 4 months, she suggests to her mum, 'Park in Danny's drive (nearer the edge of the close) – that would save some petrol!' Georgia is able to link distance travelled with the amount of fuel used.

Looking back with Georgia's parents

Money

Both of Georgia's parents remember her playing with real money.

Mum: *'She used to play with it all of the time.'*

I wonder when and why that began, because most parents worry that little children will swallow small coins. Her dad recalls that he had a very large bottle in which he saved any loose change. He says that Georgia was allowed to play with coins from that bottle when they knew she would not put them in her mouth. He thinks she was under 2 years. Georgia did not play with just a few coins. Her uncle remembers her carrying money around in a carrier bag and sometimes it was so heavy that she had to ask an adult to move it from one place to another. Once Georgia had experience of real money, there seemed no point in giving her anything else.

> **Mum:** *'One Christmas she got a till and we thought it was ridiculous to buy plastic money when she could just have real money.'*

Both parents also remember Georgia playing cards with the older children from the close.

> **Dad:** *'She used to play with Jennifer and Amy. They tried to teach her to play.'*

They also played other games which may have contributed to Georgia's ideas about quantity.

> **Mum:** *'When she was older, she used to play cards, schools and shops in the close. They all involved counting, sharing things out, taking things back and making lists.'*

Dividing and connecting materials

Cutting and dividing was not such a memorable part of her play, although, again, her dad remembers that she had scissors before she was 2 years old. He also remembers that it did not take her long to learn to use them. 'We held the paper stiff for her at first.' He also recalls that she liked cutting veg: 'We couldn't give her a really sharp knife so it was hard work for her – she would get fed up after 5 minutes.'

Both parents remember her displaying the divided travel brochure on the bathroom wall. Blu-tack was one of the things that was always on her low table in the living room.

> **Dad:** *'She used to spend ages in that corner.'*

When I was demonstrating to Georgia's dad how she divided space in her drawing, Georgia (aged 7 years) added a line making my rough sketch symmetrical, showing that the mathematical form is still important to her.

What Georgia learns about quantity and amount

Georgia's early behaviour in which she carries objects (often money) from one place to another and arranges the individual coins in different ways, is very similar to what Piaget describes (1951).

> *At 3 [years] 6 [months] she put some pebbles in a pail, took them out one by one, put them back, transferred them from one pail to another, etc.*

Piaget describes these sorts of actions as 'sensory motor practice games'. In other words children play them for sheer pleasure. Piaget says that these games develop when 'they become symbolic' or 'become games with rules' or 'lead to real adaptation'. We see Georgia's play become 'symbolic' when she imitates 'paying the man'. In this sort of play, Georgia builds up a story around her use of money and incorporates into her story the sharing of money, which has previously been an end in itself.

Playing games

The card game is an early example of Georgia developing the expertise to play a game with shared rules. In this case the rules are her own personal ones. Within the game Georgia reveals what she knows about numbers and values. There is the number of actual cards each person holds. Georgia definitely knows what is 'more' and what is 'less'. She manipulates the rules so that she always has more. Then there is the number value or currency of each card. She shows that at this stage she can seriate up to five.

The importance of learning to count

Piaget did not attach much importance to counting, but more recent research indicates that it is important for children to learn to count (MacLellan, 1997). MacLellan says that 'the emergence of counting in children is complex and a bit messy'. MacLellan is referring not just to the recital of numbers in the conventional order, which can be learnt parrot fashion, but to a real understanding of how to count. We can see that understanding developing in Georgia towards the end of her nursery time. Experiences in all areas of her life contribute to her understanding of number.

Carruthers (1996) argues that young children develop ideas about number in the same way that they develop ideas about literacy. She says,

> *Numbers exist in the child's world from birth and they are gradually building up a meaning for number and how it fits into the whole pattern of life.*

EXPLORING IDEAS ABOUT SIZE AND FIT

When Georgia explores size, her concern is with filling a space or area and whether one object will fit inside or around another object.

Georgia is completely engrossed, at 2 years 8 months, when she picks up a small perspex container (approximately 5 cm × 4 cm).

> *She tries various things in the container eg photo, fold-up toothbrush, none of which would fit. She spotted a piece of paper, which was already folded in half. She picked it up, unfolded it and looked at it, then folded it in half again, then in half again, then again and put it into the container and closed it. She looked pleased with herself.*
> (Parent Diary)

(At this stage Georgia seems happy with the action of putting something *inside* a container.)

Georgia spends the next 2 months folding and enveloping everything possible. She folds her pictures and paintings and carries a bag full of things, has money in a purse inside a box and sits on her truck, with pram attached, blanket draped over the pram and wearing a hat. (Georgia is happy to cover anything, including her head with a hat.)

Months later, at 3 years 3 months Georgia is more concerned with what can fit through a narrow space, when she says to her dad, 'Better shut the window. The rain's only small, can get in there'. Georgia now understands that rain going through the window depends on the window being open.

That summer, when the family are on holiday, Georgia spends a long time playing with laces and a wristwatch. She is interested in fastening and unfastening, as well as in what will fit. She is 3 years 6 months.

> *Georgia spent the best part of an hour fastening and unfastening my watch. She put the watch on her wrist, round her leg, round her ankle without sock pulled up then with sock pulled up. Talked a lot about watch and parts of it, speculating about whether it would fit.*
> (Parent Diary)

Georgia has refined her earlier enveloping behaviour and is more concerned with fitting.

Exploring friendship bracelets

The trend in the close is friendship bracelets. Georgia has observed how to make them during social interactions with older children, who have made them for her and each other (Schaffer, 1996). Two weeks later, Georgia has one on each wrist made for her by the older children. In the following observation, Georgia is at home and attempting to make friendship bracelets.

> *Georgia is 'trying' to make friendship bracelets. She has three pieces of embroidery thread knotted together and spends most of her time cutting one piece of thread and then the other two to even it up.*
> (Parent Diary)

Georgia is obviously very involved and talks all the way through, though, her mum says, she expects no reply, as her sentences all run into each other. This is some of her accompanying language.

> **Georgia:** *'Want a little one for Harry? How little Harry needs. I need to just cut. This is small enough Mum?'*
> **Mum:** *'Very small.'*
> **Georgia:** *... Mummy want me to cut this for Harry? Want these three colours for Harry? Think it's all right. Dad, you could help me do a bracelet? I can't do it. I can do ...'*
> **Dad:** *'You need it quite long.'*
> **Georgia:** *'You can do it that small? That going to be mine. Dad, I'm going to give you some – not that – that's my favourite. You're allowed that for him (piece of thread) ...'*

Georgia pursues this interest for at least 3 weeks. At the same time as Georgia is exploring wrapping thread or laces *around* objects, she is also interested in *distance* and in extending her own body to reach things 'with tiptoes and without tiptoes'. This may indicate that the unravelled state of the thread is equally important to her investigation as the enclosure she makes when she wraps it around an object. Georgia may be grappling with the idea of the length of the thread being 'equivalent' to the 'breadth of the enclosure' (Athey, 1990). Athey suggests that,

> *Mathematically this schema is extended in the primary school in activities such as measuring around wrist, waist, ankle and various kinds of perimeters.*

Georgia chooses stories

Georgia chooses stories which relate to ideas about size and listens to them over and over again. Two favourites are:

- *Papa Please Get Me the Moon* (Carle, 1986), a storybook containing a ladder which unfolds to reach the moon and a story in which ideas about the waxing and waning of the moon are explored.

- *Where's My Teddy* (Alborough, 1992) in which a boy loses his teddy and finds a giant teddy, which belongs to a huge bear. The anomaly is resolved when they swap teddies.

Symbols on clothing

At 3 years 7 months, Georgia knows about the symbols on clothes labels that denote sizes and is clear that she wants to be bigger rather than smaller.

> *Georgia went to show Ian her new vest which, I told her, was aged 5–6. I then asked her to try on some trousers from last year.*
> **Mum:** *'I think these should fit, as the label says they're 3–4.'*
> **Georgia:** *'No, I need 3–5.'*
> (Parent Diary)

Journeys

Georgia is also interested in larger distances. At 3 years 8 months, when they are visiting her great grandmother, she suggests going 'to Asda as it's nearer'. She also knows that 'Safeway is nearer' if they are at home. (This is accurate.)

At nursery, at 3 years 11 months, Georgia uses collage materials in the workshop area and fits materials into a defined space.

Measuring and fitting

> *We measured a picture to frame it – I helped Georgia. I then sent her to measure another picture.*
> **Georgia:** *'It measured two threes.'*
> (Parent Diary)

Georgia fits lolly sticks into a space

Georgia at 4 years has an idea of what measuring is, at this stage. She knows that it involves a tape measure and numbers. She may also understand why we measure things.

At 4 years 2 months Georgia's concern when writing names is fitting words into a space. (See Chapter Three.) Also at 4 years 4 months, Georgia went to bed with paper, ribbon and scissors in order to wrap something after watching her mum wrap up a gift for a friend. Wrapping objects with paper requires skill in measuring or estimating the size of paper needed and in folding and securing parcels.

When Georgia is 4 years 5 months, Steph brings a Doctor's bag to nursery. Several children play with the instruments. When they are putting everything back into the bag, Georgia picks up a stethoscope, saying 'If I can get it in' and 'I don't think I can get it in'. It did fit in. Georgia is estimating whether she thinks something will fit before trying it.

Looking back with Georgia's parents

Georgia's interest in size and fit seems to be rooted in her early experience with the large bottle of coins that her dad was collecting.

> **Dad:** *'She was interested in which coins would go into the bottle. 2p coins would not fit, so she could have those.'*

Georgia rarely plays with jigsaws at nursery but her dad says that 'she loved her inset jigsaws' at home. In those, the task is to fit the correct shape in the space, so it is about matching for size and shape.

> **Dad:** *'She had several of that type of puzzle and because I worked for a toy firm, I was able to keep giving her different ones from work.'*

When Georgia is 2 years, she has an inflatable globe and she becomes interested in the comparative size of countries.

> **Dad:** *'She would ask about the countries she had heard of, eg, Is England bigger than America?'*

Georgia has a tape measure, which is usually well extended.

> **Dad:** *'For months she took it everywhere – she liked opening and shutting it.'*

Looking at size labels

Both parents remember Georgia looking at size labels on clothes. In fact she still does.

> **Dad:** *'She went shopping a lot with her mum and probably saw her doing that . . . also, because of Harry's allergy, we both had to read labels on tins etc, more so than most people.'*

He feels that Georgia 'gives attention to detail' and also that she wants to be grown up.

> **Dad:** *'Georgia can't wait to grow out of shoes so that she can get the next size.'*

What Georgia learns about size and fit

It appears that when Georgia is enveloping everything in sight, this covering of objects and parts of herself, leads to 'higher order notions such as volume and capacity' (Athey, 1990). Athey suggests that if practitioners are aware of this possibility, then content can be introduced that has 'a *specific capacity*'. Athey suggests 'a picnic basket design to take specific crockery and cutlery'. She says that 'Toddlers *heap* objects but so do older children if more appropriate materials are not available'.

Using her whole body

There is very little mention in the records of Georgia's spatial awareness in relation to her whole body, except that she practises handstands and enjoys swings at the park. Davies (1995) reminds us that,

> *In the movement world of young children size is normally associated with extension ... 'Near', 'far', 'big' and 'little' feature prominently in the learning of young children and therefore their experience of this area is vitally important.*

When Georgia extends her body to reach with tiptoes and without, she is using her own body as a tool to measure. Similarly, trying on a watch with and without her sock pulled up is helping Georgia to measure and compare sizes or fit. It is not surprising that she takes up the idea of making friendship bracelets so enthusiastically. Vygotsky might view the making of friendship bracelets to be in the zone of Georgia's proximal development at that time (Lee and Das Gupta, 1995). Initially, Georgia needs a fair amount of help with making bracelets, but gradually the adult or older child can withdraw and allow Georgia a greater level of control.

Examining Georgia's progress

One could argue that Georgia's awareness of the possibility of fitting an object inside another object does not progress much from age 2 years 8 months, when she folds paper to fit inside a perspex container, and age 4 years 5 months, when she says that she does not think the stethoscope will fit in the Doctor's bag. However, at 2 years 8 months, she is trying things out, some of which obviously do not fit. At 4 years 5 months, she is thinking and can mentally construct ideas about the available space and the object that is supposed to fit. She is confident enough to express her considered opinion, even though that opinion turns out to be incorrect.

EXPLORING IDEAS ABOUT TIME AND CHRONOLOGY

While Georgia is interested in and pursues ideas about quantity, size and fit, she devotes much of her energy towards trying to grasp and understand time concepts. Georgia, like most young children, uses language associated with time concepts long before she understands the full meaning of them. What is most remarkable about Georgia is her persistent quest for meaning.

The records show that she refers to time in role play situations before trying them out in real situations. At 2 years 5 months, Georgia refers to '5 minutes' and at 2 years 8 months when she is making a pretend phonecall to her dad she tells him she will be home in 1 hour.

Harry is 4 months and Georgia is 2 years 8 months when she says that *he wore the jumper that she is wearing when he was a little baby*. (This indicates that she is unclear about the chronological order of events. She may be confusing ideas about now – is he actually wearing something that was hers when she was a baby?)

As a baby and toddler, Georgia is not a good sleeper, frequently waking during the night. This may be the source of her concern with time. Georgia is 2 years 8 months and wakes at 6.15 am.

> *Her dad told her it was too early to get up and gave her a watch to look at and told her when it would be 7 o'clock. She said 'Not see the watch – dark in the way'.*
> (Parent Diary)

Having an advent calendar at 2 years 10 months feeds Georgia's interest in the sequence of events, though, like most young children, she is not ready to wait a whole day for each chocolate.

> *Choc missing from 21st window (tomorrow). Georgia said, when asked where it had gone, 'Not me know me eat it'!*
> (Parent Diary)

At 2 years 11 months, Georgia begins to make her own meaning of time and distance. Her mum tells her that Peterborough (where Thomas the Tank Engine is) is 'only about half an hour in the car, like going to Northampton'.

> **Mum:** *'Georgia nodded and said to herself "Just about 1 minute, near Corby".'*

The important factor for her may be that it is near Corby, where she lives and, therefore, she can go to visit it.

Linking time and size

Just after her third birthday, Georgia links time and size. She compares her size and Harry's with the size of a new baby. She says, 'Next year me be four – have four candles'. She tells her grandmother that '1 hour is not a long time'.

At 3 years 2 months, Georgia is much more specific about time.

> **Georgia:** *'Last night I stayed up till 8 o'clock. Should go to bed at half past 6. Mummy let me stay up.'*

Georgia knows the number labels of significant times of day.

Linking time and distance

A few weeks later Georgia and her mum see Nicola, one of the older girls from the close, in Kettering sitting on a wall outside the shopping centre. Georgia wants to know why Nicola is sitting on the wall. Georgia's mum explains that she is probably waiting for her parents to take her home. Georgia is puzzled and says 'She might walk home'. Her mum explains that it is a long way (7 miles) and would take a long time. Georgia hazards a guess 'About half an hour?' Her mum replies 'About 2 hours.' Georgia repeated 'About 2 hours', then said 'about 4 hours'. Initially, Georgia is puzzled about why Nicola who, to Georgia, is grown-up, is waiting for her parents to take her home. Georgia's thinking is challenged and through being challenged, it is possible for 'cognitive change' to occur (Nunes, 1995). The discussion shows Georgia's preoccupation with time. This is the aspect she immediately latches on to and begins thinking about and speculating upon.

Thinking about future time

After Georgia's third birthday, she frequently refers to 'next year'. When she is 3 years 3 months, she is visiting Alison's family group at nursery. It is James' fourth birthday and the children are having a cake with four candles to celebrate. Georgia says 'I think he's four'. Her mum says 'like you'll be next year'. Georgia says, 'Is it next year already . . . for James?' This gives us an interesting insight into Georgia's thinking. It seems as if she is describing time moving towards individual people, rather than people moving towards points in time.

Georgia is 3 years 4 months.

> **Georgia:** *'Can I go to school?'*
> **Mum:** *'This September you'll go to nursery, then next September you'll go to school with James and little Emma.'*
> **Georgia:** *'Can Harry come to school with me?'*
> **Mum:** *'Harry will be going to playgroup when you go to school. You'll be four and a half and he'll be two.'*

Georgia seems satisfied with the explanation. In this instance Georgia is asking for information that she seems to be ready to understand. Talking about the future indicates some level of understanding about future events (Nunes, 1995).

Linking age and size

On the same day, Georgia talks about which days her grandmother goes to work and how old her grandmother is. She links age with size. (This time she looks back in time rather than forward.)

> *Pointed to Harry on a photo – said he was 'about 5 months'. And that she was 'about one 'cos that dress doesn't fit her now'.*
> (Parent Diary)

Georgia begins to play with ideas about age when she is 3 years 6 months. It is her great grandmother's birthday.

> **Georgia:** *'I'm four.'*
> **Gran:** *'I thought you were three and a half?'*
> **Georgia:** *'I had my birthday – it's today!'*

Each close person's birthday seems to stimulate Georgia's thinking about time and age.

Georgia is still 3 years 6 months when she uses the word 'yesterday' correctly in context and comments to her dad 'me say that right'. She has an awareness that up to then she has not used 'yesterday' correctly.

In the parent diary, her mum describes Georgia as having 'an obsession with time, distance, dates etc.'

Making comparisons

Georgia is 3 years 7 months when she has her first of many conversations about why Steph is going to be 4 years old before her.

> **Georgia:** *'Steph is three or four?'*
> **Mum:** *'Three – nearly four. I think she'll be four in October or November.'*
> **Georgia:** *'When me going to be four?'*
> **Mum:** *'January the 26th.'*
> **Georgia:** *'Me going to be four first?'*
> **Mum:** *'No you're not.'*
> **Georgia:** *'Why is Steph going to be four first?'*
> **Mum:** *'Because she was in her mummy's tummy before you were in mine.'*
> **Georgia:** *'Why?'*
> **Mum:** *'Because her mummy was pregnant before me.'*

Two weeks later and Georgia is still asking why Steph was born before her.

> *Georgia is still very interested in why Steph is four before her. She wants to be four first. She just keeps asking why Steph is going to be four before her – each answer given is replied to by Georgia with 'Why?'*
> (Parent Diary)

Georgia is not satisfied with the explanations she is given. Nathan Isaacs (1930) collected information about children's 'why' questions and from his data, said that children from about 4 years ask 'why' and that we continue to do so into adulthood. The need to ask 'why' occurs as a result of 'a sudden gap, clash or disparity between our past experience and any present event'. This information about Steph really throws Georgia's current ideas and expectations. She is challenged by the information and continues to ask 'why' until she gains an understanding of why Steph's birthday is before hers.

Georgia begins asking more questions about future time. At 3 years 8 months, just after starting nursery, she asks her mum 'When will I be six or seven?' Her mum replies, 'In 3 or 4 years time.' Georgia comments on each chunk of time: 'That's long or not long.'

Linking age and height

At nursery Georgia stands on some steps and says 'Look at me – I'm about six'. She is linking age and height.

Four weeks after Georgia's first conversation with her mum about Steph, she is 3 years 8 months and is asking about her mum's lived age.

> **Georgia:** *'You are eleventeen?'*
> **Mum:** *'No.'*

Georgia: *'Six?'*
Mum: *'No.'*
Georgia: *'20?'*
Mum: *'No – I've been 20.'*
Georgia: *'When were you 20?'*
Mum: *'6 years ago.'*
Georgia: *'That was about 1 minute ago.'*
Mum: *'No – 6 years ago.'*
Georgia: *'6 minutes ago?'*
Mum: *'No – 6 years ago.'*
Georgia: *'20 years ago?'*
Mum: *'No – 6 years ago.'*

Georgia seems to be trying to grasp the quantity and the measures of past time. She is trying to 'generate' more information about the past (Nunes, 1995).

Extending lengths of time

When Georgia is 3 years 9 months she is still working on understanding real time and how it is measured. She has had a sleep during the day and asks if she can get up for a while after going to bed.

> *I said she could get up for 20 minutes if she went back with no bother when I told her to. She moaned 'That's not long.'*
> **Mum:** *'Well, either 20 minutes or 10 minutes or nothing.'*
> **Georgia:** *'20 is more than 10?'*
> **Mum:** *'Yes.'*
> **Georgia:** *'Okay then, 20 minutes.'*
> (Parent Diary)

This seems to be about staying up as long as possible.

Georgia uses a similar strategy at nursery when it is her turn for the favourite bike. Whatever length of time she is offered, she tries to haggle for longer. When the adult says '10 minutes or 5 minutes?' she says, 'Okay, 10 minutes.' It is not always about prolonging the actual time, as she sometimes offers it to the child whose turn is next, before the 10 minutes is up. It may be about testing the limit – 'What is the longest time I can have?'

When Georgia is just 4 years, she asks 'When is Nanny going to die?' Has Georgia discovered that the limit of life is death?

Locating events in time

At 4 years 2 months, Georgia has a conversation with her grandmother about birthdays and schools.

> **Georgia:** *'When is your birthday?'*
> **Gran:** *'October.'*
> **Georgia:** *'Will I be at school in October? Is it still April? Will it be May after April? Will it be Harry's birthday the first day of May? Is Craig at Danesholme school? (Craig is a friend who has just left nursery to start school.) How long has he been going there? Will I be at school all day?'*

We can see that Georgia now has much clearer ideas about the order of months and seems to be grasping the idea of events being located in time.

Georgia still incorporates time into her role play. She has been to work with her mum (who is doing telesales) and subsequently represents what her mum does.

> **Georgia:** *'Hello Lindsey, sorry to ring you back in 10 minutes. Eismann Frozen Foods – would you like a catalogue?'*

This is an example of social context leading learning (Moll, 1990).

In May, when Georgia is 4 years 3 months, her uncle comes back from India and describes to Georgia the animals he has seen, including 'monkeys on the street'. Again, Georgia takes up a time theme.

> **Georgia:** *'Which day did you see them?'*
> **Paul:** *'Every day.'*
> **Georgia:** *'Sunday?'*
> **Paul:** *'Yes – Sunday.'*
> **Georgia:** *'Tuesday?'*
> **Paul:** *'Yes – Tuesday.'*
> **Georgia:** *'Your birthday?'*
> **Paul:** *'Yes.'*
> **Georgia:** *'My birthday? How old are you?'*
> **Paul:** *'24.'*
> **Georgia:** *'Are you older than Mop?'* (Mop is his mother.)
> **Paul:** *'No.'*

Paul explained that he is 20 years older than Georgia and that his mum (Mop) is about 20 years older than him. Georgia is still attempting to locate events in time.

At nursery when Georgia is 4 years 4 months, she uses watercolours and is interested in how quickly the paint dries. In this instance, Georgia has a sense of how long paint takes to dry and she is surprised when it dries more quickly than usual. Her sensitivity to issues about time makes her notice and comment on the speed of drying.

Georgia and Steph begin to get a sense of their own history when they look at their Celebrations of Achievement (nursery record book) together.

> **Georgia:** *'Is that a good one? Do you like that one? I haven't got that jumper any more. That was my first day at nursery. I started writing.'*

Georgia is now able to think about and to reflect on her own process of learning and her own past.

Looking back with Georgia's parents

Georgia's parents were both aware of her interest in time concepts. Neither had really thought about how it started. Her dad says that he is 'a light sleeper' and would be up with Georgia 'six, seven or eight times during the night' when she was a baby. Naturally both parents would discuss in the morning what sort of a night it had been. So there would have been a great deal of conversation *about time* when Georgia was a baby. Alongside this, Georgia's mum liked to have a routine. So naturally Georgia was brought up with a sort of structure to her day. It is difficult to know whether routine suited Georgia as a unique individual, or whether she got used to it because of her early experience. She and Harry are very different and her dad says that 'Georgia really needs routine' even now at 7 years. Whatever the source of her interest, Georgia wanted to know about the sequence of events that were going to happen.

Giving Georgia a sense of time

> **Mum:** *'I tried to give her a sense of what real time is. I reassured her when I left her in creche. I would say "I'll be one and a half hours – it's not a long time – have good fun".'*

Georgia would want to know when Ian would be home.

> **Mum:** *'I think it is that she's looking forward to seeing him and wants a sense of how long to wait.'*

Georgia became *obsessed* with time, wanting to know how long it would take to get to places and how her mum knew how long it would take. Her mum took her questions seriously and would time journeys, telling Georgia as each minute passed.

> **Mum:** *'I knew she wanted to understand – that's why I used to time things.'*

Timing events in the close
Georgia explored some time concepts in the close.

> **Mum:** *The children used to play handstands and see who could stay up the longest, counting in seconds. Even if Georgia wasn't doing it, she was watching the older girls.'*

One of her favourite toys was a cart, which she played with in the close.

> **Mum:** *'That was all about experiencing weight, speed – who could pull it fastest – how fast they could go without it being dangerous and tipping over.'*

Explaining how events are located in time
Georgia's most memorable question for both parents was why Steph was going to be 4 years before her. Her parents tried to explain it in concrete terms to her by making a calendar.

> **Mum:** *'When she was going on and on and on about Steph's birthday being before hers, after explaining lots of times, we made a sort of calendar. It went from January to December with little pictures to signify when it was in the year eg snow in January. Then we wrote on it whose birthday was when. Georgia's is in January so I explained that hers came first in the year – she had already had hers for this year but Steph was just about to have hers. She still wasn't happy.'*
> **Dad:** *'She just thought it wasn't fair! By the following year, it wasn't a problem – she seemed to understand.'*

Georgia (at 7 years) has been reading about Isaac Newton and is interested in when he died and how long he lived. There is a chronological list of events at the end of the book and this interests her. She understands that the events described in the book occurred 300 years ago and that it was around the time of the Great Plague.

What Georgia learns about time and chronology

Georgia was interested in and intrigued by two separate aspects of time concepts – 'order' and 'duration'. The ability to put things into a logical order is important in all areas of life. Bancroft (1995) says,

> An understanding of the temporal concepts of 'order' and 'duration' is crucial to our ability to plan and organise as well as to our ability to understand things like stories and to solve problems where order is important.

Piaget carried out research into children's understanding of time. When he carried out clinical observations, he found that children have difficulties with the concept of time until they are in their tenth year (Bancroft, 1995). However, there is evidence in his naturalistic observations of his own children, that they were interested in time and using related language from the age of 2 years.

> . . . between 2 [years] and 2 [years]; 6 [months] she understood the length of time indicated by: 'in a minute,' 'just a moment,' etc.
> At 3 [years]; 10 [months] L asked, in reference to that day, which she had been told the day before would be 'to-morrow': 'Is it to-morrow in Pinochet (our district) or is it to-morrow everywhere?'
> J at 5 [years]; 9 [months]: 'Are there times when there aren't any hours, or are there always, always hours?'

This partial understanding of and interest in time has been observed in a more recent study by Bancroft (1985). He says that,

> . . . there was some evidence that these children were talking about time concepts from the beginning of their third year.

Like Georgia's understanding of it being 'next year already . . . for James', it is a sort of time and space problem. Time is such an abstract concept that young children must be struggling with what it is and where it is. It is important for children to ask questions over and over again, as there are several related concepts for them to grapple with.

Learning language related to time

Georgia learnt time-related language, such as the words for units of time, days and months. Vygotsky would say that the words are important. To him each word is 'a generalisation' and therefore already 'a thought' (Vygotsky, 1962).

In other words, when Georgia expresses ideas using words, she is already thinking and conceiving ideas about what she is expressing.

Georgia's sequencing of days and months became clearer when she was over 4 years and, from what her parents say, her development caught up with what she wanted to know about 'why Steph was four before her' by her fifth birthday!

Summary

Georgia's mathematical explorations and questions related to:

- quantity and amount, division and parts of whole objects

- size and fit

- time and chronology.

She was persistent in her search for understanding, often wanting to achieve or understand to the same extent as the older children she spent time with.

We have now looked at how Georgia's mathematical understanding developed. In the next chapter we will be looking at how Georgia develops her understanding of scientific concepts.

5 DEVELOPING SCIENTIFIC CONCEPTS

Our actions in everyday life require that we take into account the physical world.
(Nunes, 1995)

Children are born passionately eager to make as much sense as they can of things around them . . . Children observe, they wonder, they speculate and they ask themselves questions. They think up possible answers, they make theories, they hypothesise . . .
(Holt, 1989)

The scientific concepts that Georgia is most concerned with from the ages of 2 to 5 years are:

- food allergy

- childbirth

- changes in state.

Georgia, like any other child in the world, is part of the society in which she has been born. Her quest for knowledge of that world is determined by a number of factors:

- Her particular interests and the circumstances in which she finds herself are important.

- Georgia seeks and gains knowledge about her world that is at times very specialist and at other times more general.

- Georgia is free to discover some properties of materials by experimentation.

- Other information she seeks by asking questions.

- Some information is vitally important for her parents to share with her. Information connected with her younger brother's food allergy comes into this category. Her brother, Harry, has several severe reactions to dairy products and other foods, which are potentially life-threatening.

Scientific concepts about food allergy

By the time she is 3 years 6 months, Georgia appears to have an understanding of what causes her brother's allergy. She takes it for granted and rarely mentions it unless it is necessary. During a conversation about her grandmother's birthday the subject comes up.

> **Georgia:** *'Have a small cake for Harry, cos he's not allowed eggs or chocolate.'*

She is most interested in checking or in pretending to check the ingredients of products. At 2 years 9 months she seems to know what she is looking for on the side of a carton, but then announces, 'It's from Safeways.' A year later, at 3 years 9 months, she sees her dad looking closely at a pot of fromage frais.

> **Georgia:** *'You are looking to see if Harry's allowed that? You looking at ingredients?'*

At 3 years 5 months she is confident enough to play with and to joke about the information.

> **Mum:** *'If she has something she doesn't want him to have, she'll say ''It's got eggs or milk in!'' whether it has or not!'*

Looking back with Georgia's parents

Her parents do not, at the time, see Georgia as having specialist knowledge. However, in retrospect, they realise that what the family discovers about her brother, constitutes knowledge that most adults do not possess. The first signs of the allergy appear when Harry is 6 months and Georgia is 2 years 10 months, although he has always been a sickly baby. Therefore, her interest in reading the carton at 2 years 9 months does not stem from her parents' anxieties about ingredients, but is already an interest of hers. Before Harry's allergy is diagnosed, there is a period of uncertainty. Initially the doctor thinks the swelling around his face might have been caused by a different fabric softener, as the family have been to a friend's wedding and stayed overnight in an hotel. Although they do not directly discuss this with Georgia, she is around when it is mentioned and is aware of her parents' anxieties. Once the diagnosis is made, however, she has to know the rules immediately.

Dad: *'It was important that she knew because she loved fromage frais and we had to tell her not to share hers with him.'*

Mum: *'We also had to tell the other children in the close. Things like Wotsits and frommes are easy to eat when you are little.'*

Georgia is sometimes in situations where she has to tell adults.

Dad: *'She was aware of the symptoms and could relate to an adult what was happening and knew to get help.'*

Mum: *'We had been in a lot of situations where other people did not know and would share out food . . . or children would leave drinks on the floor.'*

It seems to me that her parents have high expectations of Georgia at 3 and 4 years, but they are clear that she has to have the information. The alternative is very little freedom for them to even be in a different room for a matter of seconds. Her parents feel it is right to tell her and to expect her to tell others if necessary.

Mum: *'I think the more trust you give, the more trustworthy they become. The allergy may have set up a context in which she was given trust and responded positively.'*

Of course it is a gradual process.

Dad: *'She had shown in her understanding that she knew.'*

She is able to practise what she knows at home and in the close where the family live. Almost everyone here knows about the allergy. It is an extremely dangerous and serious situation and not one with which they can take risks.

Mum: *'She was really doing it, not playing at doing it.'*

At almost 5 years, Harry has outgrown his allergy, but Georgia, at 7 years, can still remember the problems.

Georgia: *He weren't allowed to eat some things like cheese . . . his eyes and mouth would swell up . . . I'd tell you . . . he'd go to hospital.'*

Georgia's scientific knowledge about allergies

So what is the nature of scientific knowledge that Georgia learns about her brother's allergy? She has enough factual information to know not to explore the situation by giving him different foods. She is not free to solve any part of the problem. Her parents welcome her questions and are happy to explain and repeat the facts as many times as necessary. They want her to link what he eats with the result. Therefore, it is not enough to focus on the different 'states' of her brother's health: 'well' and obviously 'ill' with swollen head and eyes (Das Gupta and Richardson, 1995). She needs to understand the process and the relationship between the products he eats and his resulting reaction.

Helping Georgia to link cause and effect

Georgia has to know that a negative reaction is *caused* by eating certain foods. She needs to know about the raw products he is allergic to but she also needs to know that it is not always obvious which products contain the problem foods. She needs to know, for example, that chocolate contains milk. So, not only does her brother's appearance change, but, food products that look different can contain some of the same ingredients. These are complex ideas and Georgia seems to cope with the important aspects. The emotions experienced by Georgia and her parents each time Harry shows signs of the allergy may contribute to her ability to remember. Carter (1998) says that 'events that happen in a state of emotional excitement' are likely to be remembered easily and over a long time.

SCIENTIFIC CONCEPTS ABOUT CHILDBIRTH

The birth of Georgia's younger brother, when she is 2 years 3 months, provides a scientific context in which she is likely to gain some general information about babies and childbirth. Georgia's parents are aware that the birth of her sibling gives them an opportunity to show her books with illustrations about how a baby grows and is born, as well as stories which explore the emotional aspects of a baby being born into a family.

Her brother is 7 weeks and she is 2 years 5 months when her parents notice that she takes a special interest in three books which deal with issues about new babies joining the family.

> *Suddenly wanting three books about expected baby and baby's arrival. Likes saying 'Walter' and repeats the name several times.*
> (Parent Diary)

(Walter is the name of a baby in one of the stories).

Noticing differences

Georgia is interested in the physical differences between herself and her brother. When Georgia is 2 years 7 months, she jokes about physical features. Her parents connect this with 'the fact that she changed Harry's nappy yesterday'.

A few days later Georgia makes an announcement.

Georgia: *For Christmas I want a boy dolly that can wee out of his willy.'*

Around this time Georgia (2 years 8 months) frequently plays mummies and babies. She explores different roles.

Georgia, Nicola and Samantha were all playing at Samantha's house this week. Georgia got the buggy she wanted and also a doll and said 'I Colette (mum), this Harry (pointing at doll) and Georgia at playgroup.'
(Parent Diary)

The schemas that Georgia explores extensively during this period seem to link with her later understanding of how babies are born. She puts objects inside other objects which are capable of covering them completely. Athey refers to this action as 'containing' and 'enveloping' objects or oneself (1990). Georgia tries covering or putting objects inside containers using all sorts of different materials. She is 2 years 9 months when her parents record that 'She put a coin inside a tea infuser and shook it'. The infuser is spherical, can open and close, and can contain and conceal small objects. The concealed object rattles when shaken proving that the object is still inside though it cannot be seen. Babies inside wombs are also concealed.

Mum: *'She does a lot of wrapping up coins at home, also getting her bag ready (in buggy and wrapped up).'*

Wrapping coins conceals them with flexible covering, just as skin stretches with the baby still inside the womb.

A week later Georgia is still exploring these themes.

She is well into enveloping. Lots of babies in pram, buggy and truck. Carrying a bag full of things (looked quite big and heavy). When I asked what was in it, she said 'nappies and things'.

Had money in purse, inside box . . . Wore hairband, then a bit later hat . . . then a different hat. Sat on truck with pram attached and blanket draped over pram wearing hat.
(Parent Diary)

These explorations of envelopment seem to help her to understand one function or purpose of covering or enveloping objects, animals or people, often babies.

Exploring going through a boundary

Another schema which Georgia investigates is going through a boundary. This exploration helps her to understand how an object inside a container comes through to the outside of the container. This relates to the actual passage of a baby from the womb to the outside world.

At 3 years 1 month Georgia is worried 'About her teeth – "Just bleeds a little bit".' She is concerned with blood coming through her gums. The blood is not apparent until it comes through the gum.

At 3 years 2 months, 'Georgia is very interested in Harry's arm – he has had a blood test.' She is interested in the actual breaking of the skin. One of her ideas is that the tummy is cut open to allow the baby to come out.

> **Mum:** *'She was using the outside tap and watering can. She poured lots of water into the chimney pot (plant pot).'*

The watering can is a container with a spout, so that when it is tipped up the contents come out. The properties of liquids are suitable for pouring. A less flexible material might not fit through the spout. A baby is not liquid and does not seem very flexible, therefore it is difficult to imagine it coming through a space much smaller than itself.

> **Georgia** (3 years 3 months): *'Better shut the window, the rain's only small, can get in there.'*

She is differentiating according to size and displaying her understanding of what stops the rain from going through. Again, she is thinking about and estimating what will fit through a space. A baby cannot fit through a small space.

What a 'dead end' is

At 3 years 4 months Georgia becomes interested in what prevents a clear passage through a boundary. She wants to know what a 'dead end' is. Her mum drives her to the end of a cul-de-sac to show her. On the same day, she makes a representation of a 'dead end' when she is painting.

Later that day at her grandmother's house, Georgia plays with earrings.

> **Grandmother:** *'She liked putting earrings in my ear – gave her a huge sense of satisfaction – did each about 20 times, putting them in, putting the back bit on and taking them out.'*

Georgia is gaining firsthand experience of putting rigid material through a small space. Interestingly, a hole in an ear lobe looks almost invisible when there is no ring through it. The baby goes through a small space – is there a parallel?

A month later Georgia is 3 years 5 months.

> *Georgia is playing at the table with colour pegs . . . Talks about pushing them right down and pressing them right down. Frequently turns pegboard over.*
> (Parent Diary)

She uses force and gravity. Both force and gravity are used in childbirth. She is able to co-ordinate ideas about containing and going through at 3 years 6 months.

> *She played in the sand with sand tray toy placed over a dumper truck. She filled the container, which was on top, with sand, then opened the 'plug' and the sand went through to the truck.*
> (Parent Diary)

One way of containing then releasing an object or some material is to use a plug. Perhaps the human female has a plug or trapdoor, which when removed, releases the baby?

Her earliest interest at nursery at 3 years 7 months, is woodwork, particularly hammering nails through wood. She continues to pursue this interest for several months. Again, she is using force and the weight of the hammer. A powerful force might push the baby out.

Pushing things through

Georgia (3 years 11 months) at nursery, is playing with dough.

> *Georgia starts pushing dough into the dough train (works a bit like a garlic press). She pushes the handle down and, as the dough comes through, she looks at me and says 'Look!'*
> (Family Worker Observation)

With this tool she can see and experience a mass which is solid but flexible, pushed through a space smaller than itself. This is similar to what actually happens during the birth of a baby.

A few minutes later, she compares dough with earrings, clearly showing that she is interested in the going through action.

It is 3 months later, after gaining the necessary conceptual knowledge, when visiting the hospital where she and her brother were born, that she begins to show a real understanding about how a baby is born. She is 4 years 2 months.

> *. . . we passed the maternity unit and I told Georgia that the last time I'd been there, it was for Harry to come out of my tummy and that it was where she had come out of my tummy.*
> *Georgia asked 'Do they cut your tummy open and get the baby out?'*

(She offers her own theory.)

> *(I just assumed she knew how babies came out, as she'd seen all my pregnancy books when I was having Harry.)*
> **Mum:** *'No, they come out of your gina.'*
> **Georgia:** *'Out your gina? Out your gina?' (in amazement at the top of her voice!) 'The baby comes out of your gina?'*
> *I then explained about caesareans and Georgia said, 'But why would they cut your tummy if you could just push it out your gina?'*
> (Parent Diary)

This statement shows that at this stage she could think about and construct a mental model of the process.

Looking back with Georgia's parents

Georgia's parents are aware that, although they have told her how babies are born and have shown her several well-illustrated books about the birth, it is a long time before she has an even partial understanding of the process. They assume that going to antenatal clinic with her mum, looking at books together and being prepared to answer her questions around the time of her brother's birth, helps her to understand.

Her dad recalls very little information about her question. Her mum feels that she asks questions mostly about the 'historical' aspects.

> **Mum:** *'She wanted to know what she weighed, where she was weighed and measured – gory details like the blood etc.'*

> **Georgia** (at 7 years): *'Was I 45 centimetres and he was 54 centimetres – cos they're the same numbers the other way around?'*

This is totally accurate showing that the questions she asks at the time are important to her and that she has retained that information.

> **Georgia:** *'Mum – why do some people be born late? Harry was born 13 days late and I was born 1 day late.'*

Again this is accurate. When we discuss these aspects, Georgia also offers more information.

> **Georgia:** *'I don't play mummies and babies anymore. I stopped when I was six.'*

Georgia's scientific knowledge of childbirth

Before Georgia can understand how a baby is born, it appears that she has to be able to think of the womb as a container with the growing or expanding baby contained inside. The period when she envelops various objects, some flexible and others inflexible, helps her to partially understand. However, it is only after exploring a going through a boundary action schema, that she is able to co-ordinate and 'mentally construct' (Athey, 1990) ideas about a birth. What is not clear is 'how much experience is required for a new form to be constructed'. The other issue is that she is given the factual information much earlier, at a stage when it appears she is unable to understand it. Does the factual information in fact contribute something to her later understanding? Vygotsky would support the idea that instruction and information should be offered ahead of development (1962). This also raises questions about the importance of always having reference books available to children, which may support their own explorations and discoveries with accurate information and illustrations.

SCIENTIFIC CONCEPTS ABOUT CHANGES IN STATE

Georgia is interested in experimenting with materials, noticing and causing changes, particularly in consistency, as well as noticing when a material or person changes its appearance. She often plays with sand and water in the garden, but a holiday at the seaside when she is 2 years 5 months gives her the chance to experiment further.

> *Visit to beach – Georgia most interested in picking up lumps of very soggy sand on a spade and throwing it into the water.*
> (Parent Diary)

A lump of soggy solid disappears and appears to dissolve in the large mass of liquid.

During the next few weeks, she enjoys 'watering the flowers' in the garden each time she visits her grandparents. Liquid poured on soil disappears.

In November at 2 years 10 months, she notices something new.

> **Mum:** *'She could see her breath outside – she went to the front door, blew and said "smoke", then came into the room and did the same and said "no smoke"!'*

Georgia is observing the transformation from gas to liquid.

Around Christmas, at 2 years 11 months, Georgia paints, using poster paints and water colours.

> *She partially enveloped the paper with paint, starting in one corner and adding different colours, which blended together . . . she used water colours, trying each in turn, making a separate mark on the paper with each . . . she said, 'Look at the colours I've oozed' and spoke about 'navy-blue'.*
> (Parent Diary)

This could be an interest in how colours change when blended with other colours.

She visits nursery at 3 years 3 months and is involved in melting chocolate to make krispie cakes. This explores the transformation from solid to liquid and back to solid.

Later the same day, Georgia pours lots of water into a chimney pot containing plants.

Georgia: *'It's okay, it's melting.'*

It is disappearing but making the soil soggy. The liquid appears to be changing to a soggy solid state, which has a similar consistency to melted chocolate.

Mum: *'Georgia told me a boy had put water on her hair.'*

She is feeling the effect of liquid on her hair, which absorbs the liquid in a similar way to the soil.

At 3 years 4 months she was most interested when her dad was throwing away a tub of margarine. The bottom of the tub was covered in a sheet of ice.

Georgia: *'Why are you throwing it away?'*
Dad: *'Because the fridge was up too high and it's frozen.'*
Georgia: *'That's why you making glass.'*

Georgia has noticed that water turns to ice, so once again liquid becomes solid. She compares it with glass which is also solid and transparent.

Watering flowers

She continues to water the flowers and reveals her interest in the quantity of water and its effect when she is 3 years 4 months.

Georgia: *'Look how many water. That gonna make it grow quicker.'*

She has an interest in the effect of water on seeds, which will change by becoming bigger.

Georgia (3 years 4 months) continues to explore and to understand the effects of water on other materials.

Georgia said, 'It's raining – my slide's wet!'
I said, 'You'd better slide down to dry it.'
Georgia, No – I can't because my bum will get wet!'
(Parent Diary)

The liquid on the slide will be absorbed by the material of her clothes and it will penetrate the material reaching her skin. The liquid will disappear.

Wetting and soaking materials and people

Georgia becomes interested in soaking materials, including other people and herself. She is on holiday at the seaside, aged 3 years 6 months.

> *Splashed herself and me as soon as possible. Kept telling me she wouldn't splash me but then did. I said she wasn't allowed to get wet. She sat down in the water in her clothes and then sang, 'We are soaking and we not allowed to get wet!'*
> (Parent Diary)

There was also the aspect of being able to experiment more freely at the seaside because of the space and feeling free to enjoy what was available, because of being on holiday. She has firsthand experience of being dry and becoming wet.

A month later, at 3 years 7 months, she plays with a water gun at home.

> **Georgia:** *'Can I get my hair wet? [pause] It's soaked already!'*

Again, she is having firsthand experience of being dry and becoming very wet.

Soaking with paint

Three weeks later, Georgia is painting.

> *Georgia painted some computer paper. She used mostly red paint and rotated the brush to get lots of paint on it. 'It's all wet – it's soaking.'*
> (Parent Diary)

By now she really knows what 'soaking' means. Dry paper is soaked with paint.

When Georgia starts nursery, she has opportunities to use a wider range of materials. She frequently plays in the workshop area with glue, paint and other materials. She becomes concerned with the opposite of being soaked, that is the process of liquid drying. This may indicate her interest in the *'reversibility'* of operations (Richardson, 1995). She discovers that liquids dry out when spread thinly over certain materials. She is often more involved in picking the dried-out glue off her fingers, than in producing a picture or model. When she is 3 years 9 months, she takes nail varnish from home to nursery, puts it on her own and other children's nails, then picks it off. Again she is exploring liquid to solid.

At 3 years 10 months, Georgia spends most of her time in the wet area painting and picking paint off her fingers

Allowing paint and glue to dry

Two weeks later Georgia enjoys using clay.

> *Georgia manipulated the clay, adding water to it, before putting a candle in it. She slowly filled the clay with sequins and glitter. (She took her candle-holder home when it dried out.)*
> (Family Worker observation)

Georgia is examining the change from damp clay to malleable soggy clay to dried out clay.

She often uses paint, applying it in different ways to different materials.

Changing her appearance

It may have been pure coincidence or possibly part of her predominant enveloping schema, but Georgia frequently swaps clothes with her friend Stephanie around this period. Sometimes she changes into nursery clothes for no reason. She tends to choose clothes that are too small or particularly old, thereby changing her appearance.

Cooking to transform ingredients

At her grandparents' house, she enjoys transforming ingredients by cooking. She likes to make things that involve the transformation of liquids to solids.

At nursery, at 4 years 2 months and 4 years 4 months she uses Modroc (discovering the properties first and still exploring its use later on. This is a Plaster of Paris bandage used to set broken limbs which turns from solid to liquid and back to solid.

At 3 years 11 months Georgia is preoccupied with dough. She is particularly interested in dividing dough using a knife, garlic press or dough train. She is combining dry and wet ingredients to make a malleable solid.

At 4 years Georgia's preferred material is peat.

> *Georgia became totally involved in mixing peat and water for over an hour this morning. The peat was with the pulleys. She did not bother about the pulleys, but began putting handfuls of peat from the ground into a bucket and asked if she could add water. (The transformation/consistency seemed to be the important part for her.) She said she was making 'pasta'. She was adding liquid to solid particles.*
> (Family Worker Observation)

At home, at 3 years 9 months, Georgia is using crayons.

> *She did a picture by colouring all over a piece of card with a crayon then wiping it with a damp cloth and then using another crayon. She spent quite a while experimenting – trying to rub off the crayon etc. (She did both sides with different colours).*
> (Parent Diary)

Crayon resists water unlike some of the absorbent materials she has used, so in this case the liquid does not disappear.

Transforming the living-room

At 3 years 11 months Georgia likes being involved in transforming the living room.

> **Mum:** *'Georgia was ill and got up in the evening when we were changing the room around. She offered suggestions about where to put pieces of furniture.'*

This does not involve matter changing state but from Georgia's point of view the effect may be similar. It is not surprising that she wants to direct.

Taking the decorations off the Christmas tree at 3 years 11 months also captures her interest.

> **Georgia:** *'We undecorated the tree today!'*

Is this an interest in reversing a process? Some transformations are not reversible. Again she is making something physical look different.

At 4 years, she wants to know 'Why are some people black and some white?' Does she think that people change from one to the other?

Also at 4 years, she describes what she thinks is happening when she puts her hand under the tap as the water is warming up.

> **Georgia:** *'This water's getting lumpy!'*

In this case the water feels as though it is changing from liquid to solid.

At 4 years 4 months, she helps make cakes.

> **Georgia:** *'Dad you can have your cake soon – when it's dried out.'*

Looking back with Georgia's parents

Georgia's parents are less aware of her consistent interest in changes in state. Quite a lot of her investigations are carried out at nursery when she is 3 years 7 months or more and it is only when we view all of the material as a whole that we recognise how often her explorations link with her subsequent knowledge about changes of state.

> **Dad:** *'She was always interested in the cold weather . . . in water turning to ice. She always wanted water in the sand . . . we had the sandpit from when she was two.'*
>
> **Mum:** *'Did her interest in changes in state link with her brother's allergy?'*
>
> **Georgia** (7 years): *'I still like picking glue off my fingers . . . Last year there was ice over the sandpit – I thought it was strong, so I stepped on it and it broke.'*

I am interested in what she knows about reversibility. I ask her about whether glue ever becomes liquid again.

> **Georgia:** *'No'*
> **Me:** *'What about ice to water?'*
> **Georgia:** *'Yes.'*

Her mum remembers her liking a book about water. It is a reference book with factual information about how water evaporates, becomes ice and so on.

Georgia at 7 years stands by her theory about more water making plants grow more quickly.

Georgia's scientific knowledge about changes in state

Georgia's scientific experiments about changes in state are of two main types:

1   Adding water of varying amounts to other materials.
2   Spreading or sprinkling liquids and allowing them to dry out.

Her scientific method consists of:

- Asking herself 'what if I do X?', for example wet my clothes or hair?

- 'Y will happen' – she is developing a hypothesis, that the liquid will disappear.

- Then carrying out experiments to test her hypothesis by varying the variables: adding different amounts of liquid, different types of liquid to different types of material.

Holt (1989) says that 'real learning is a process of discovery' and that children '*make*' knowledge. Georgia initiates the experiments and is also sensitive to events in the environment which relate to her central concern. For example, occasionally she observes the effect of heat or cold being applied to liquids. She shows great interest in these effects. Georgia appears to be exploring change, both external and internal, reversible and irreversible. She is certainly interested in the effect her actions have on materials, as well as on other people. Piaget views very young children as displaying a 'rigidity of thought' (Miller, 1992). This is characterised by their inability to think in a flexible way. For example a very young child might see a coat 'held in a hand', then 'hung up' and be unable to understand or to think about how it stays near the wall. It is not unusual to see young children holding their coats near a coatpeg as though something magical may happen. When children begin to show an interest in the *transformation process* rather than the *beginning state* and *end state*, this is highly significant. At this stage they begin to understand that 'the coat staying against the wall' depends on 'the loop surrounding the hook'. Athey (1990) believes that this interest in cause and effect directly precedes 'conservation', that is, a full understanding that a quantity or number stays the same, even though it is distributed differently, unless anything is added to it or taken away from it. During this period Georgia seems to be systematically exploring,

- what happens to different materials when they become wet

- what happens to different materials when they are soaked with water

- whether glue always dries when spread thinly

- whether other liquids dry when sprinkled or spread thinly.

An important aspect of experimenting with and focusing on the process of change is the discovery of which procedures are reversible and which are not.

SUMMARY

The main thrust of Georgia's scientific explorations and discoveries from 2 to 5 years relates to:

- understanding and communicating information about her brother's food allergy

- seeking information about childbirth by asking questions about aspects which she is ready to learn about

- exploring and discovering knowledge about changes in state by firsthand experiences and the manipulation of materials

- her strong schematic concerns are often the source and the means by which she generates new ideas

- what happens for her, is firmly rooted in her experience in her family at that time and never to be replicated again.

In this chapter we have looked at the source and development of Georgia's scientific concepts. In the next chapter we will be looking at Georgia's emotional development.

6 GEORGIA'S EMOTIONAL DEVELOPMENT

Our passions, when well exercised, have wisdom; they guide our thinking, our values, our survival.
(Goleman, 1996)

> We will look at Georgia's emotional development through:
>
> • her spontaneous interest in power issues and her use of power
>
> • her actions and reactions during periods of change, uncertainty and transition

We have already seen that Georgia is very much a 'people person'. The relationships she makes, as well as the relationships she observes and hears about, are central to her development and learning. Georgia learns about the world through people. Two of Gardner's 'multiple intelligences' are:

• to understand other individuals

• to understand ourselves (1991).

For Georgia, people seem to be the essential element in any learning environment. Part of what she learns is about relating to others and understanding and expressing her own feelings and thoughts. Like any young child, Georgia begins by struggling to understand and gain control of the world as she sees it (Stern, 1985).

POWER ISSUES AND GEORGIA'S USE OF POWER

Like other aspects of Georgia's development and learning, her emotional development does not take a simple, linear route. She is influenced by the people she knows and loves and by their actions and experiences. According to Piaget (1951) children have 'general schemas' about people, based on the people they know. They will 'tend to assimilate all other individuals' into this general schema. Given Georgia's early and sustained relationships with older children, it is not surprising that she seems to have a view of older and bigger people as more powerful than her.

Who has power?

When Georgia is 3 years 3 months, she asks her dad a question about his relationship with his boss, Kai, which puzzles both parents initially.

> **Georgia:** *'You follow Kai about at work?'*

Georgia's query about how people relate to each other at work becomes clearer when she is cross with her mum and says (in a rebellious tone), 'I'm going to follow Steph about!' (Steph is her friend at creche and playgroup.) The inference is that Georgia (in order to punish her mum) is not going to use her power to do something of her own choosing, but will take on the subordinate role of following Steph. Two other related statements add to our understanding:

1 **Georgia:** *'Gemma follows us about.'* (Gemma is new to playgroup and clings to Georgia and Steph.)
2 **Georgia:** *'We been following baby Daniel about!'* (Again at playgroup, Georgia and Steph play with the idea by following someone who is obviously less knowledgeable than them.)

These two statements illustrate Georgia's understanding of the processes of learning as experienced by other children. Georgia knows that it is a silly idea for her to do what a much younger child ('baby Daniel') does, but she does it for fun. Bruce (1991) says that humour 'involves knowing something so well that it is possible to play with your play'. Georgia is in a powerful position when she knows something so well that she can turn it upside down for fun. Her question about Kai seems to be an attempt to discover more about her dad's relationship with Kai. If younger, less experienced children like Gemma at playgroup, follow older children about, then is that what her dad does at work?

Using power

Georgia (at 3 years 5 months) is 'ill and stroppy' and desperate to use whatever power she has.

> **Georgia** to her mum: *'You not coming to my birthday then!'*

She says this quite often when she's not happy with someone. The situation becomes quite humorous.

> **Georgia:** *'You can come to mine birthday then but you're not going to have any cake!'*
> **Mum:** *'But I'm going to make the cake.'*
> **Georgia:** *'I don't care anyway!'*

Georgia uses a similar threat a month later (at 3 years 6 months) when she falls out with her grandmother. Her grandmother goes along with her decision to choose who is invited to her birthday.

> **Gran:** *'I'll have to send your present then . . . and the postman will bring it.'*

Georgia immediately becomes interested in what the present will be and changes her mind, saying 'You can come to my birthday.'
   This acceptance of Georgia's decision defuses the situation completely.

Dominating others

On two occasions Georgia tries to dominate children who are younger than her. At 3 years 5 months, Georgia is playing with James, who is 3 months younger and lives next door.

> *I told her to ask James' mum if he was allowed some sweets – then she could choose them at Safeway – this was to appease Georgia as she didn't want to come with me. A bit later, Georgia to James: 'You allowed hard or soft?'*
> *James, 'Hard.'*
> *Georgia, 'No, you're not.'*
> *James, 'Soft.'*
> (Parent Diary)

In this instance Georgia has the power and is going to abuse it by giving James no choice. She may be behaving in the same way that she experiences older children or adults behaving towards her at times. Does she always know and understand why she is not allowed something? Is she always given genuine choices that she understands? Or does she just realise that, in this instance, she is more powerful than James? Georgia may be using the situation to 'exercise' her power (Goleman, 1996).
   At 3 years 8 months, Georgia is playing upstairs in her bedroom with Laura (who is 6 months younger) when there is an argument.

> **Georgia:** *'I wasn't letting Laura out of my room 'cos I wanted her to play mummies and babies and she didn't want to.'*

In this instance Georgia is trying to force Laura to play her choice of game. Georgia's more usual companions are older rather than younger than her. Georgia may be struggling to negotiate with a younger child. Pollard (1996) describes some of the negotiations which go on at school between teacher and pupils, as well as at home between parents and children or siblings. He says,

> *In general, adults have the power to initiate, assert, maintain and change rules, whilst children must comply, adapt, mediate or resist.*

Strategies for joining other children at play

When Georgia is 3 years 6 months her parents write down in the Parent Diary her range of strategies for joining other children at play.

> *With Harry or Laura, she takes over or tries to get him or her to do what she wants. She says things like,*
> *'. . . want me to show you . . .'*
> *'. . . want me to do . . .'*
> *'. . . want to do this . . .'*
> *Outside in the close she will just watch until asked to join in (if the older children are playing an actual game) or say, 'Me have a turn?'*
> *If the children in the close are just hanging around or all doing different things she'll just go and join in by doing similar things nearby.*

This shows that Georgia already has a range of adaptable strategies for getting along with other children. She takes the lead with younger children. With older children, she tries to assess what kind of play they are engaging in, before either asking whether she can follow their lead or replicating what they are doing alongside them, in order to make a smooth transition into their play. With younger children, Georgia is the initiator. With older children, she wants to join in and discover what they are playing.

Power to express feelings

Around the same time, Georgia is confused and seems powerless to express her feelings.

> *She fell over when demonstrating hopping. Immediately her mood changed, she looked down, fiddled with her T-shirt. She looked cross and unhappy and did not want to speak to anyone. (3 years 6 months)*

> *She wanted to sit in the back of the car. The seatbelt is only effective with her carseat in the front. Was very stubborn and kept refusing to go in the front – eventually I told her she had to. (3 years 7 months)*

(Grandmother) I babysat because Ian was late. Both children were tired and upset.
Georgia tore up the writing which she had done for me. Was distraught till she said
she wanted dummy and Nancy and I said that was fine. (3 years 9 months)
(Parent Diary)

Georgia has just started nursery. Her dad has changed jobs and her mum begins
working evenings. There is more tension within the family than usual. Things
are less predictable than previously. Georgia is able to 'soothe' herself with her
dummy and Nancy (Goleman, 1995) and in choosing to do this, seems to restore
some of the power she feels is slipping away from her (Winnicott, 1975).

At nursery the staff encourage children to choose where, what and with
whom to play. Georgia is happiest when she is near adults or children whom
she already knows. Rutter (1992) says 'familiarity tends to be associated with
interactions that are better meshed, more complex and which involve more
fantasy'. Pollard (1996) observed a child in his study as 'more self-confident and
relaxed' when alongside a peer.

At nursery Georgia exercises her power in different ways:

- by participating in family role play (3 years 9 months)

- by choosing a different Family Worker when Alison is off (at 3 years 10
  months)

- by choosing what to wear (at 3 years 9 months), particularly enjoying
  transforming her appearance – she can anticipate her mum's reaction to her
  altered appearance.

At 3 years 11 months, Georgia throws her dummy in the bin after advice from
the dentist.

Becoming empowered

The nursery staff are proactive in offering the older children small group
sessions on:

- friendships and conflict

- bullying

- physical boundaries

- strangers

- good feelings and bad feeling (Mars et al, 1990).

Georgia participates in all five sessions and is happiest discussing these issues when Steph is alongside her.

Looking back with Georgia's parents

Both parents remember Georgia's dummy and Nancy being really important to her. She always had to have them with her when she was very young. Once, before Georgia was 2 years, she lost Nancy

> **Dad:** *'Losing Nancy was the most traumatic 2 days of her life – and ours, because we knew she wasn't going to sleep without Nancy.'*

Her parents were able to replace Nancy after 2 days by contacting the person who had bought her and finding out where Nancy came from. Georgia ended up with two Nancys – an identical one from the supplier in Germany and a larger one donated by an older child, who had received it as a gift from the same person that gave Georgia hers. Georgia (at 7 years) still has both dolls and sometimes takes one of them to bed with her.

The power of complex play

Georgia has close attachments to Aunty Eloise and Jennifer, as well as to her parents and brother. However, her parents feel that the balance of power in these early relationships, is not the same as the balance of power in subsequent peer relationships.

> **Dad:** *'She always had Jennifer and Amy.'*

We have seen in Chapter One that the twins liked Georgia to be the baby and also that they might 'give in to her.'

> **Mum:** *'She had to learn to negotiate – even with Steph and Laura – they weren't going to give in to her.'*

Her dad noticed that at nursery 'She tended to stay with Steph – they knew what they were going to do.' This fits with the view of Rutter and others (Tizard, 1986) that 'more complex' play develops when children know each other well.

The power to destroy

When Georgia destroys her writing, she is using her power destructively. This is something that happens only rarely when Georgia is very distressed. Her parents remember this.

Dad: *'She screwed a picture up a couple of weeks ago because we didn't have something she wanted to use on it.'*

Her mum feels that she can 'usually stop her from destroying her work' by talking to her about what she is doing and discussing why.

The power of humour

Georgia is at her most powerful when she displays her sense of humour. It was in a spirit of humour that she would deliberately change into nursery clothes that were too small or did not suit her. Her mum is aware that 'she purposefully chose clothes she knew I would hate – it really amused her.' This is a little like 'playing with play' (Bruce, 1991). In this instance she is aware of her mum's opinions and attitudes about how she wants Georgia to dress and look. Rather than take these opinions seriously, Georgia is able to poke fun at her mum and is confident that her mum will see the funny side of the joke too.

Georgia's use of power and her emotional development

It is important for babies and young children to form 'attachments' with the people who care for them (Schaffer, 1995). Georgia formed 'several attachments' with adults and older children who responded sensitively to her. Those attachments form a secure base from which to explore and take risks. Rutter says that 'secure attachments' are the 'key to good relationships' (1992) and 'foster autonomy rather than dependency'. Georgia clearly feels most powerful and able to explore and take risks when she is alongside an adult or child she knows well.

The humour Georgia uses is interactive. It is shared with others she knows well and dependent on 'in-group knowledge and familiarity' (Rutter, 1992). Laughter is beneficial in all sorts of ways. Goleman (1996) says that even 'mild mood changes can sway thinking'. Laughter encourages a positive outlook and creative thinking. It is 'the ratio of positive to negative emotions that determines the sense of well-being'. Although, at times Georgia struggled to express her hurt, this was balanced by her ability to find or create humour, which she shared with close friends and family.

The power of mastering problems

Dweck and Leggett (1988) have put forward the idea that children generally react in one of two ways when faced with challenging tasks. They either see themselves as inadequate failures and display 'helplessness' or they relish the challenge and display what they call 'mastery-oriented' behaviour. A child who is being helpless will very quickly give up, but a child who relishes a challenge will believe in themselves, persevere and generally be more in control of any situation. Georgia's outlook generally was positive, but her confidence became a little shaky at times. We have already seen that she had some strategies for 'soothing' herself. Those strategies also seemed to involve Georgia in being able to use her power. There were small choices that Georgia could make, for example, when she needed the comfort of dummy and Nancy, who to be near at nursery and so on. We shall see in the next section what happens during periods of uncertainty and change.

PERIODS OF CHANGE, UNCERTAINTY AND TRANSITION

In Chapter One we saw that Georgia was born into a very stable family:

- two parents who had lived together for some time before her birth

- a father in a steady, well established job

- a close, supportive extended family

- friendly neighbours in a small, intimate close.

Georgia, as an individual, has a sociable temperament and her early environment seems to suit her. We are now going to look at what happens when change occurs within that stable environment.

The birth of Georgia's brother

The first major change in Georgia's life is the birth of her brother, Harry, when she is 2 years 3 months. We have already heard that Georgia liked looking at reference books about how babies grow and are born (Chapter Five). Her parents spend a lot of time explaining what will happen and how things will change. She seems to take all of this in her stride. Harry is 2 months when her parents notice Georgia *suddenly* exploring stories 'about expected baby and baby's arrival'.

This sudden rekindled interest takes her parents by surprise. However, as human beings we need to 'assimilate' and 'digest' new information (Piaget, 1951). Stories can enable us to express our feelings and to identify with other perspectives (Barnes, 1995). Life has changed for Georgia and maybe, at this point, she is beginning to realise that Harry is here to stay.

Georgia continues to react positively towards Harry but is nasty towards her mum quite often when Harry is a baby. She may be 'displacing' her confused or angry feelings by punishing her mum, who she is certain will always love her, rather than hurting or showing her anger towards Harry (Isaacs, 1933).

Starting playgroup

At 2 years 7 months Georgia starts playgroup. The transition seems to be smooth but Georgia must be thinking about where Harry and mummy are when she is at playgroup. At 2 years 8 months Georgia explores these issues through role play.

> *Georgia, Nicola and Samantha were all playing at Samantha's house this week.*
> *Georgia got the buggy she wanted and also a doll and said 'I Colette, this Harry'*
> *(pointing at the doll) 'Georgia at playgroup'.*
> (Parent Diary)

Whitehead (1997) says that 'the experiences children bring to group settings must be re-enacted or tried out in many different symbolic ways'. Role play and stories are two of the ways in which Georgia explores her changing world.

Harry's allergic reaction to dairy products

The next major change is Harry's allergic reaction to dairy products. This happens, for the first time, when Georgia is 2 years 10 months. Unlike Harry's birth, her parents cannot prepare her for this. They cannot offer an explanation about the cause. All they can do is reassure her that it is not her fault and that Harry will be all right. The records do not show any negative or unusual reactions from Georgia during this period of uncertainty, which lasts several months. It is reasonable to suppose that Georgia was aware of her parents' anxiety. Miller (1992) says that young children 'are sensitive to their parents' state of mind'. There are several factors which may account for the Parent Diary showing no change in her behaviour:

- Her parents are so focussed on Harry that they take less notice of Georgia and write less in the diary?

- She recognises their anxiety and understands that it is about Harry and not about her?

- She trusts her parents' power to make things okay?

- She can see the reaction – it is physical and, therefore, tangible?

- Her parents discuss the allergy in her presence and, therefore, there is no hidden agenda?

- Her attitude to Harry is positive and, therefore, she is less likely to feel she is to blame in any way?

Dunn and Kendrick (1982) found that,

> If the mother talked to the first-born about the new baby before the birth, relations between the siblings were much friendlier by the time the baby was 14 months than they were in families where this did not happen.

So maybe the time given to discussing the baby with Georgia before the allergy was discovered, contributes to her understanding and interest in his state of health when he has a reaction.

By the time Georgia is 3 years 5 months the allergy has been diagnosed and the family know what to do in an emergency. When Georgia is 3 years 6 months her mum has written in the Parent Diary that she sees Georgia most involved in 'pretend games – going to the doctor's, doing cholesterol tests and writing prescriptions.' Georgia is almost certainly playing out some of her fears to 'make them bearable' (Piaget, 1951) and to put them behind her.

Georgia's transition to nursery

Georgia's transition to nursery is not as easy as her parents expect. She displays her ambivalence before she starts nursery by refusing to go to creche. A combination of changes occur around the time that Georgia is starting nursery. Her dad changes his job for a second time and her mum begins evening work. This changes the pattern of care. What actually happens is that sometimes her dad cannot get home in time to take over, so he has to ring their grandmother, who rushes over to care for the children until he arrives home. We have already heard from her dad that Georgia likes to know what is going to happen. So a sudden change of arrangement, at a time when Georgia is already coping with several changes, results in her feeling angry and powerless.

Georgia has also possibly held on to her negative feelings for several months while Harry's allergy was the focus of attention. The resulting behaviour may be a reaction to an accumulation of feelings (Goleman, 1995). It does not seem a coincidence that her favourite stories at this time are *Angry Arthur* which is the

Georgia and Steph having a story

story of a child whose anger explodes, and *Avocado Baby* which is about a baby who becomes incredibly strong and powerful through eating avocado each day. She listens to these stories several times both at nursery and at home.

Georgia's reactions, even throughout this period of change, were not extreme. At nursery, she would be clingy and stay near adults rather than becoming involved with other children. Rutter (1992) points out that 'children are most likely to cling when they are frightened and upset'. At home she would sulk or cry if she could not have what she wanted. There was less flexibility than normal. Georgia was not willing to 'make compromises'. If we were to use Laever's indicators of well-being, we might notice that, at times, Georgia's well-being was lower than usual.

Just after Christmas, when Georgia is 3 years 11 months, her dad is made redundant and is out of work for 2 months. Her mum switches to morning work. There is some friction between her parents. Georgia's mum sees this redundancy as an opportunity for her to work full-time. Georgia's dad does not want this solution and is determined to resolve it by finding a new career. During this time the effect on Georgia at nursery does not seem very great. At home, at 4 years, she draws a picture of the whole family.

> **Georgia:** *'Daddy's angry.'* (His features were all scrunched up – like a frown).

Strategies for settling at nursery

Georgia still finds it difficult to separate from her parents when she arrives at nursery, but has developed some strategies, which help her feel more in control of the situation.

- She chooses a particular adult – Georgia becomes friendly with Angela as well as Alison.

- She brings something from home to use as an object of transition, usually a toy.

- One day, when she feels particularly vulnerable, she wears a sunhat all morning (even though it is February).

Georgia's dad starts work again when she is 4 years 1 month and a period of stability follows.

Georgia begins to be unsettled again about a month before leaving nursery to start school and shows this by behaving differently and unco-operatively. This time, her parents recognise the signs and realise that she needs help to express her feelings of fear and uncertainty about the impending change.

Looking back with Georgia's parents

Georgia's parents realise that around the time of Harry's birth and the discovery of the allergy, they had very high expectations of Georgia.

> **Mum:** *'I think we expected her to be grown-up when we had Harry. We expected emotional maturity and she was only two.'*

Georgia's parents feel that her close friendships were important to her throughout periods of change and transition.

> **Dad:** *'She's more sociable than Harry. She learnt a lot from the older children – she was never bored when she was with them.'*
> **Mum:** *'She became friendly with James the year before school – then they were in the same class when they started school.'*

Georgia (at 7 years) remembers her friends at nursery.

> **Georgia:** *'Me, Stephanie and Laura played together.'*

I remember Georgia's concern with Steph's age, asking 'Steph's a bit older than you?'

> **Georgia:** *'She's 4 months older than me.'*

(Some things stay the same despite other changes.)
   Both parents remember Georgia participating in role play.

> **Mum:** *'I remember her being the sister.'*
> **Dad:** *'She liked being the baby – she loved being pushed around in a buggy or cart.'*

Georgia learns to express her fears
Georgia's mum realises that big changes, like leaving nursery to go to school, are difficult for Georgia.

> **Mum:** *'She's grotty if there's any change – I tell her "I used to be scared" – and once she realises that I was scared of starting school, she changes her attitude. She still won't express it verbally, but her behaviour will change after we have explored it.'*

Her parents did not realise that sometimes their worries had an impact on Georgia.

> **Mum:** *'When Ian was out of work for 2 months, we probably did not realise that Georgia would be worried about Ian not having a job.'*

After reading this chapter, Georgia's mum adds that 'when Ian was made redundant, there was a real power struggle going on between us. Georgia would have witnessed those negotiations and experienced some of the friction'. Power was an issue for the parents. Is it a coincidence that Georgia was interested in power?

Georgia enjoys being pushed around in a cart

A year after this power struggle, Georgia's parents separated. Her mum moved into her own house a few months later. The way her parents have handled this and have explained to the children what is happening and why, has been crucial in ensuring their well-being. Negotiating what is best for the children has been paramount.

Learning to negotiate

Georgia seems to find it difficult to back down, when she is negotiating.

> **Mum:** *'The other night I said I'd read a chapter of her book – it was only three pages, so she said she didn't want it at all. She backed down, in this instance, after I explained to her that she could ask for more (nicely), that she was cutting off her nose to spite her face and she would miss out on what she wanted, and that it was okay to back down and have what she really did want.'*

Rather than being prepared to negotiate for the best deal she can get, sometimes Georgia will give up or be inflexible.

> **Mum:** *'She did the classic with her birthday – wanted more children for Dinomites than we were prepared to pay for. She knew we would not give in. I explained why and what she could have. She said she would not have anything. She wanted to have 20 children at £4 per head. We said 10. She said she would contribute her money – £11 – I said we would put £1 to it and have another three children. That still was not good enough. It is as if she cannot back down.'*

Although Georgia's parents live separately, they are only a couple of closes apart and the children spend time each week with each parent. This makes it even more important for the parents to have a consistent approach.

Georgia adds, during the discussion, 'If I asked dad, he would' implying that she thinks her dad might back down.

However she has loyalties to both parents. Although she would like 20 children to her party, she ends up choosing something completely different.

> **Mum:** *'She has ended up with a sleepover for two friends.'*

Georgia can choose which house she has her sleepover.

I ask Georgia, 'How do you get ideas for what you want for your party?'

> **Georgia:** *'I read a book called* The Sleepover Club *– they sleep over at each other's houses.'*

Towards the end of our discussion, her mum is reflecting.

> **Mum:** *'Is her being able to deal with change about me telling her that I understand why she feels like that and that I feel like that sometimes? . . . that only happened after we split up and I was very worried about her.'*

How Georgia learns to cope

Georgia can cope with small changes, in fact some events she finds exciting and stimulating. It seems that when several things change simultaneously, over which she has no power, that everything becomes confusing and overwhelming. Miller (1992) advises parents that 'giving something a shape and talking it over can be a help'. This is what Georgia's mum has learnt to do over the years.

Georgia herself seems to use role play in a therapeutic way. Faulkner (1995) says that the 'themes of children's play can tell us about their developing social knowledge and also about their emotional fears and anxieties'. Children can control what happens in their play in a way that they cannot do in real life.

Making small choices

When Georgia is feeling particularly vulnerable even small choices seem to restore her confidence. Roberts (1995) sees 'acceptance' as 'the heart of self-concept'. Maybe if those around you accept your instinct to be near a familiar person, to carry something from home to nursery or to wear something you wore as a younger child, then you truly feel accepted and valued as the person you are on that day.

In her studies Dunn (1984) acknowledges that there is 'pressure on a firstborn to "grow up" and be independent because there is now a baby'.

Parents often do this without realising it. Georgia's parents realise that they had high expectations of her. Her mum also comments that, because of what she has found works with Georgia in relation to impending change, she now tries to offer Harry the opportunity to talk through his fears and anxieties. This shows that as parents and workers, we can learn from the children we get to know, as we go along.

SUMMARY

1   Georgia explores the use of power over others and shows an interest in hierarchies and relationships at work. Attachments to others, the use of humour and a mastery-oriented approach to learning are investigated.

2   Georgia copes with change and transition by:

- participating in role play

- using stories to explore feelings

- transporting objects of transition from home to nursery.

We have now explored some aspects of Georgia's emotional development. This concludes our exploration of Georgia's learning through four subject areas. In the final chapter we will conclude by making links across the subject areas and paying particular attention to how learning in one subject affects learning in other subject areas.

7 GEORGIA'S STORY — MAKING CONNECTIONS

Everything about the child's development links and enmeshes. Feelings, thoughts, physical movement and spiritual life are all part of the 'whole child'.
(Bruce et al, 1995)

At the beginning of this book, we were thinking about how Georgia and other young children seek to make connections between their experiences. After introducing Georgia and her family, we considered her progress in different areas. Although we looked at each subject area separately, Georgia often explored the subjects simultaneously. It was important to her that they were connected and not isolated from each other.

In this final chapter we will look at:

- how we can help Georgia to connect the different things she learns

- Georgia starting school

- Georgia as she is now – her friendships, interests and what she likes to do

HELPING GEORGIA TO CONNECT

Georgia's world seems to be held together by relationships. Georgia's relationships with other people and her interest in the relationships of others, seems to make up the integrating mechanism which pulls together her feelings, actions, thoughts and everything she learns.

Georgia's role play

Georgia uses role play to understand a complex world. For example, when Kai intrigues her, Georgia plays at being Kai. Being Kai entails:

- Feeling like Kai. Woodhead et al (1995) say that 'pretend feelings are at the heart of pretend play'.

- Acting like Kai – carrying things in a briefcase and making marks on paper as she thinks Kai does.

- Thinking about Kai in relation to her dad – building concepts about 'work' and 'being a boss'.

Bancroft (1995) says that,

> *Once experiences can be organised in terms of their similarity, children have the basic skills to develop* concepts.

Practising writing and transporting objects is part of being Kai. Both writing and transporting seem incidental, but at times, they are important aspects of the play. It seems that Georgia learns about writing through imitating Kai, then imitates Kai in order to practise writing.

Planning to extend what Georgia is doing

At nursery, when Georgia is interested in practising writing, we might offer her genuine tasks that involve writing and communication, for example, putting her own name in the computer book, helping to mark the register or recording in some way who has had snacks. We might introduce her to different alphabets, writing systems and languages. Looking at different languages might lead us to discover where people live, aspects of their different lifestyles and cultures. Pinker (1994) says that 'early childhood' is the 'critical period' for 'language acquisition'. Colin Blakemore (1998) says that currently, our school system is not making use of this information. Starting to learn a second language at secondary school is, in fact, much too late as the sensitive or critical period for acquiring language lasts until the age of seven. People can learn new languages as adults, of course, but may struggle with pronunciation and have to work much harder than young children do.

Accepting Georgia's feelings

Looking across the areas of the curriculum includes taking into account both emotional and intellectual needs. Roberts (1995) reminds us that 'knowledge and acceptance' are important when we are considering feelings. When Georgia was settling into nursery and feeling emotionally vulnerable, Angela (Family

Worker) used her prior knowledge of what Georgia was currently enjoying at home (making friendship bracelets) to engage her at nursery. There was a hidden message which Georgia recognised: 'this person knows and accepts me'. A less skilled worker might have tried distracting Georgia without first accepting how she was feeling.

Focussing on processes not products

This idea of knowing and accepting each child's agenda and approach means that, as adults, we focus on processes rather than products. In Chapter Five we saw that Georgia was more interested in how glue changed from liquid to solid, than in producing a picture or collage. If we have ideas about predetermined outcomes, Georgia might miss out on learning about scientific changes. We would miss the opportunity to offer her language to support her learning and other materials to add to her growing knowledge of changes in state and consistency.

Supporting Georgia's learning

Adults need to take the lead and offer rich materials for Georgia to experience scientifically (a workshop environment is best, so that children can select their own materials). We need to observe whether she can choose, note what she chooses and take it from there. It seems a little like two people creating a dance – one leads, the other follows, then offers a new step. The first responds with a sidestep, the second takes it forward in their own way, and so it goes on. If the adult takes too large a step, then the child cannot keep up. If the adult takes the dance in the wrong direction the child is left behind. It is important to stay close and keep checking out which way your partner wants to go. All too often children are not expected to be the creators, but merely the followers.

Let us take, as an example, a real scenario – Georgia (at 3 years 6 months) is playing with junk mail.

1   Georgia initiates: '. . . got big scissors and cut up paper . . . in half, in half again progressively until there were lots of very tiny pieces.'
2   Adult offers a resource to extend what Georgia is doing: '. . . an envelope to put them in so that she can take them home.'
3   Georgia extends her ideas: '. . . she cuts up any big pieces "so they'll fit" into the envelope.'
4   Adult can assess Georgia's knowledge: Georgia is dividing and is working at a 'functional dependency' level (Athey, 1990). That is, she understands

that fitting the pieces of paper into a 3-dimensional defined space (inside the envelope) depends on making them small enough to fit. She is interested in dividing and in fitting objects inside other objects.

5   Adult can offer further extensions based on knowledge of Georgia's interests: these activities can include words such as, 'fit', 'size', 'inside', 'half', 'quarter', 'eighth', 'fill' and 'seal' (Language). If unit blocks are available, this might be a good time to show Georgia the similarities between the blocks and her divided paper (Maths). Georgia might like to make simple concertina type books, which fold inside a cover (Technology). Stories can be told which include ideas about objects being inside other objects, such as *A Dark, Dark Tale* (Brown, 1992) or *The Very Hungry Caterpillar* (Carle, 1969) (Literature). Georgia might enjoy and learn from chopping up fruit for snacks and sharing it between a small group of children (Personal and Social Development). She might be interested in watching the pet hamster gather large amounts of food in its mouth (Knowledge and Understanding). Any of these offerings may be taken up or rejected by Georgia. Whatever she takes up may lead her and the adult in a new direction. The adult can, at any stage, be thinking about extending across all areas of the curriculum in order to ensure that what Georgia is offered is broad and balanced.

The environment as the source of development

When Georgia participates in role play she is practising what she sees as the whole behaviour of whoever she is imitating. At other times, for example, when she is cutting out, she is trying out aspects of what she has seen others do. We can make a comparison here with what Vygotsky claims happens in language development (Van der Veer and Valsiner, 1994),

> *The child speaks in one word phrases, but his mother talks to him in language which is already grammatically and syntactically formed and which has a large vocabulary, even though it is being toned down for the child's benefit. All the same, she speaks using the fully perfected form of speech . . .* Something which is only supposed to take shape at the very end of development, somehow influences the very first steps in this development.

Georgia's environment includes people using language, maths and every other skill and concept at a fully developed level. The 'environment', Vygotsky argues therefore, is the 'source of development'. He would say that the fully developed forms used by adults influence Georgia while she is developing and therefore drive the developmental process. The lesson we can learn is to ensure that when we offer materials in nursery, we enable children to play with them using scenarios from the real world of home and nursery. It is infinitely more important at this early stage, for children to enjoy and to understand real purposes of writing than it is for them to form letters correctly. Each child will practise in his or her own way, just as Georgia does, while continuing to be influenced by the real purposes which can be seen in the environment.

We have looked at how Georgia explored all areas of the curriculum at nursery. We are now going to look at how Georgia coped with the transition to school.

GEORGIA STARTING SCHOOL

Georgia explores the ideas about school

We heard in Chapter Three that, for about a month, Georgia wants the school leaflet as her bedtime story every night. She seems to be learning about the rules from the leaflet – what is allowed and what is not allowed! We also heard that in the close Georgia plays at 'schools' with a number of older children. She knows for a long time, prior to starting school, that James and Little Emma will be starting the same school at the same time as her. She seems intrigued by the concept of 'school' and wants to understand in much the same way that she tried to understand what Kai does at work. She plays at being at school, listens to stories about school and asks questions about school. The difference is that Georgia knows she will soon become part of the school community. The final stage for her, is expressing her fear of the unknown aspects of going to school.

Georgia discovers what it is like at school

Once Georgia has expressed her fears of starting school, she begins to look forward to the new experiences. James, who lives next door, is in the same class as her. The teacher is very important to Georgia. Her first teacher, Jean, makes friends with Georgia very quickly. Georgia's mum feels that the relationship with the teacher must be good for Georgia to be happy and to learn.

> **Mum:** *'The most important thing for me is that the teacher likes my child – I know Jean likes her.'*

Georgia fits in very easily with the school routine and is happy. She likes writing, reading and maths and enjoys meeting new people. At playtime she and James play together continuing with the play that goes on at home.

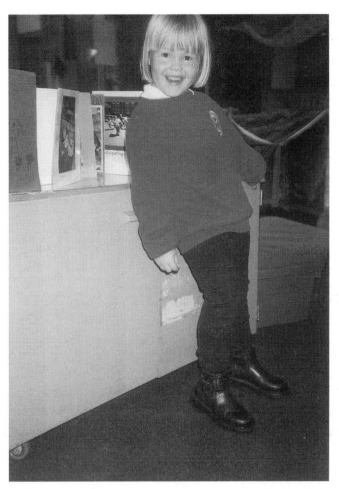

Georgia just after starting school

Again it is the 'goodness of fit' between Georgia's temperament and the school context in which she finds herself that matters (Oates, 1994). She is in the position of being alongside James, whom she has known since his birth, and surrounded by other new people. During her year at nursery she has risen to several emotional challenges, as well as exploring, discovering and practising her skills in building, using the computer, listening to stories, painting, gluing, using clay and dough and role play.

What Georgia does at home after starting school

After Georgia starts school, she continues to do the same things at home, but at a more complex level. She practises drawing and writing at every opportunity, as well as taking her schoolwork in her stride. She continues to combine drawing and writing. At 4 years 10 months she produces the piece below. This is a core with radials in the form of a house, infilled with enclosures.

Georgia still enjoys writing and drawing

Georgia is displaying her sense of humour at 5 years when she writes 'Look – mummy is not little'. She reads it aloud and hoots with laughter. The records end there, but Georgia continues to thrive at school and is fortunate to have Jean as her teacher again for her third year at school.

GEORGIA AS SHE IS NOW

Her friendships, interests and what she likes to do

Georgia is now 7 years old. She is still close to and identifies with her mum, Aunty Eloise and Jennifer. She continues to be close to her brother, Harry, though this can mean arguing and falling out, or ganging up on their parents, as well as playing together. Equity is an issue for Georgia. Although she might give in to Harry's wishes some of the time, she is now more likely to fight for equality. Georgia and Harry are very important to each other, particularly as they both spend time together each week with each of their parents. They always have each other, even though they might be missing one of their parents.

Georgia has several sets of friends:

- two close friends at school who are both girls

- friends in dad's close – all of the same children who have been there since her birth

- friends near mum's close

- children of her parents' friends.

Living in two homes

James and Stacey (his older sister) helped in the transition to the children's mum's house, as their Gran lived almost next door to the new house. Their parents allowed James and Stacey to spend time with Georgia and Harry at both houses. They also allowed them to sleep over at both houses and Georgia and Harry to sleep over at their house.

Georgia and her brother see both parents most days each week and, up to now, have spent Christmas days and birthdays together as a family. Her parents have, however, taken them on separate holidays, and although this was quite daunting the first time, Georgia seems to think this is exciting now.

Georgia's interests

Georgia's interests have not changed. She still enjoys drawing and writing and is an avid reader. She likes adventure stories and can be seen walking around with her nose in a book if the story is exciting enough for her. She often reads to Harry. At Christmas, both children made presents for the rest of the family. Georgia painted glass candle holders and made models with plaster of Paris. One of the favourite presents she received was a personal organiser into which you enter two dates of birth and the organiser tells you how compatible the two people are.

Georgia is less interested in using the computer now, though she dabbles with Harry's Nintendo. She has given up gymnastics but enjoys swimming. She likes to go and watch her mum playing netball and last summer started playing tennis with Harry, when her mum and Aunty Eloise took the children to the tennis courts with them. One of Georgia's favourite trips is to Dinomites, which is a huge softplay area for children.

Georgia's interest in people

People and their relationships still seem to be the main motivation for Georgia. She likes all of the soap operas on television. She also watches documentaries about people. A particular favourite was 'Children's Hospital', which took viewers through the traumas experienced by real children and included their surgical operations.

Georgia likes playing games like Monopoly and Yahtzee. Naturally her peer group are more important to her now. She likes clothes and pop music and has already been to a school disco.

Recently, she was very excited that there was going to be a residential trip from school. However numbers were limited and her name did not come out of the hat. She was very disappointed until she realised that her two close friends from school could not go either. Georgia likes to be challenged by her schoolwork. At home she often asks for hard sums or difficult spellings in order to practise. Recently her class have been studying natural disasters and she has been motivated to discover more information from reference books. Could it be the consequences for the people involved that interests her?

GEORGIA – A SUMMARY

- Georgia learns through imitating whole scenarios.

- We extend Georgia's learning by offering content across the curriculum to match her specific concerns.

- When Georgia starts school, social relationships continue to be her primary concern.

- Georgia continues to develop her interests through the people she knows and through her interest in people in the wider world.

APPENDIX: GEORGIA'S GALLERY

These photographs show Georgia growing in age and in confidence. As you will know from reading the text, relationships with other people are very important to Georgia. Her well-being is high when she is with her favourite people. I have included photos of Georgia with the individuals who have been closest to her during her early years.

A massage group

On holiday

Jennifer, Samantha and Georgia

Harry and Georgia

Aunty Eloise with Georgia

Dad, Georgia and Harry

Harry and Georgia

Georgia and her Mum

Georgia age 7 years

BIBLIOGRAPHY AND REFERENCES

Alborough, J. (1992), *Where's My Teddy?* Walker Books, Falmouth Cornwall.

Arnold, C. (1990), *Children Who Play Together have Similar Schemas*, Unpublished project submitted as part of a Certificate in Post-Qualifying Studies.

Arnold, C. (1997), *Understanding Young Children and their Contexts for Learning and Development: Building on Early Experience*, Unpublished dissertation, M.Ed., Leicester University.

Athey, C. (1990), *Extending Thought in Young Children. A Parent Teacher Partnership*, Paul Chapman, London.

Au, K.H. (1990), Chapter entitled 'Changes in a teacher's views of interactive comprehension instruction' in Moll, L.M. (Ed), *Vygotsky and Education*, Cambridge University Press.

Bancroft, D. (1985), *The Development of Temporal Reference: a study of children's language*, unpublished PhD thesis, University of Nottingham.

Bancroft, D. and Carr, R. (Eds) (1995), *Influencing Children's Development*, Blackwell, Oxford.

Barnes, P. (Ed) (1995), *Personal, Social and Emotional Development of Children*, Blackwell, Oxford.

Bartholemew, L. and Bruce, T. (1993), *Getting to Know You*, Hodder and Stoughton, London.

Blakemore, C. (1998), Presentation at Pen Green Conference on 'Giving Children a Sure Start', Nov 1998, Corby, Northants.

Blanck, G. (1990), Chapter entitled 'Vygotsky: the man and his cause' in Moll, L.C. (Ed), *Vygotsky and Education*, Cambridge University Press.

Bowlby, J. (1953), *Child Care and the Growth of Love*, Pelican Books, Harmondsworth.

Bowlby, J. (1958), 'The nature of the child's tie to his mother', *International Journal of Psychoanalysis*, 39, 350–73.

Bowlby, J. (1969), *Attachment and loss: Vol. 1. Attachment*, Basic Books, New York.

Bowlby, J. (1973), *Attachment and loss: Vol. 2. Separation: Anxiety and anger*, Basic Books, New York.

Bowlby, J. (1991), *Attachment and Loss: Volume 1*, Penguin, London.

Brown, R. (1992), *A Dark, Dark Tale*, Red Fox, London.

Bruce, T. (1991), *Time to Play in Early Childhood Education*, Hodder and Stoughton, London.

Bruce, T., Findlay, A., Read, J. and Scarborough, (1995), *Recurring Themes in Education*, Paul Chapman, London.

Bruce, T. (1997), *Early Childhood Education*, (Second Edition), Hodder and Stoughton, London.

Bruner, J. (1980), *Under Five in Britain*, Grant McIntyre Ltd., London.

Burningham, J. (1982), *Avocado Baby*, Jonathan Cape, London.

Buss and Plomin (1984), *Early Developing Personality Traits*. Hillside, NJ: Lawrence Erlbaum.

Carle, E. (1969), *The Very Hungry Caterpillar*, Puffin Books, Harmondsworth.

Carle, E. (1986), *Papa please get the moon for me*, Hodder and Stoughton, London.

Carr, M., May, H. and Podmore, V. (1998), Paper entitled 'Learning and Teaching Stories: New approaches to assessment and evaluation in relation to Te Whariki', Symposium for 8th European Conference on Quality in Early Childhood Settings, Santiago de Compostela, Spain, Sept 1998.

Carruthers, E. (1996), 'A young child talks numbers': A developmental link between literacy and numeracy', Paper from unpublished M.Ed. (1996), University of Plymouth.

Carter, R. (1998), *Mapping the Mind*, Weidenfeld and Nicolson, London.

Clay, M.M. (1975), *What Did I Write?* London: Heinemann.

Cohen, J.M. and M.J. (1993), *The New Penguin Dictionary of Quotations*. London: Penguin.

Daniels, H. (Ed) (1996), *An Introduction to Vygotsky*, Routledge, London.

Das Gupta, P. and Richardson, K. 'Theories of cognitive development in Lee, V. and Das Gupta, P. (1995), *Children's Cognitive and Language Development*. Milton Keynes: Open University Press.

Davies, M. (1995), *Helping Children to Learn Through a Movement Perspective*, Hodder and Stoughton, London.

Donaldson, M. (1978, 1987), *Children's Minds*, Fontana Press, London.

Donaldson, M. (1992), *Human Minds*, Penguin, London.

Dunn, J.B. (1977), 'Patterns of early interaction: continuities and consequences' in Schaffer, H.R. (Ed), *Studies of Mother-infant Interaction*, Academic Press, New York.

Dunn, J. and Kendrick, C. (1982a), *Siblings: love, envy and understanding*, Harvard University Press, Cambridge (Mass.).

Dunn, J. and Kendrick, C. (1982b), *Temperamental differences in infants and young children*, Pitman Books Ltd., London.

Dunn, J. (1984), *Brothers and Sisters*, Fontana Books, London.

Dunn, J. (1988), *The Beginnings of Social Understanding*, Blackwell, Oxford.

Dunn, J., Brown, J.R. and Beardsall, L. (1991), 'Family talk about emotions, and children's later understanding of others' emotions', *Developmental Psychology*, 27, pp 448–55.

Dunn, J. (1993), 'Studying Relationships and Social Understanding' in Barnes, P. (Ed), (1995), *Personal, Social and Emotional Development of Children*, Blackwell, Oxford.

Dweck, C. and Leggett, E. (1988), A Social-Cognitive Approach to Motivation and Personality, *Psychological Review*, Vol 95, Pt 2, pp 256–733.

Eisner, E. (1985), *The Art of Educational Evaluation: A Personal View*, Falmer, Lewes.

Faulkner, D. (1995), Chapter entitled 'Play, Self and the Social World' in Barnes, P. (1995), *Personal, Social and Emotional Development of Children*, OU, Milton Keynes.

Flanagan, C. (1996), *Applying Psychology to Early Child Development*, Hodder and Stoughton, London.

Gardner, H. (1991, 1993), *The Unschooled Mind*, Fontana Press, London.

Gelman, R. and Gallistel, C. (1978), *The Child's Understanding of Number*, Harvard University Press, Cambridge, MA.

Goleman, D. (1996), *Emotional Intelligence*, Bloomsbury, London.

Goodman, Y.M. and Goodman K.S. (1990), Chapter entitled 'Vygotsky in a whole language perspective' in Moll, L.C. (Ed) (1990), *Vygotsky and Education*, Cambridge University Press.

Graves, D. (1983), *Writing: Teachers and Children at Work*, Heinemann, London.

Greenfield, S. (1997), *The Human Brain A Guided Tour*, Phoenix, London.

Gura, P. (Ed) (1992), *Exploring Learning: Young Children and Blockplay*, Paul Chapman, London.

Henry, M. (1996), *Young Children, Parents and Professionals,* Routledge, London.

Hoffman, P. (1998), *The Man Who Loved Only Numbers*, Fourth Estate, London.

Holt, J. (1989, 1991), *Learning All the Time*, Education Now, Ticknall.

Isaacs, N. (1930), Appendix A on 'Children's "Why" Questions' in Isaacs, S. (1930), *Intellectual Growth in Young Children*, Routledge and Kegan Paul Ltd., London.

Isaacs, N. (1974), *Children's Ways of Knowing*, Teachers College Press, London.

Isaacs, S. (1930, 1966), *Intellectual Growth in Young Children*, Routledge and Kegan Paul Ltd., London.

Isaacs, S. (1933), *Social Development in Young Children*, Routledge and Sons, London.

Isaacs, S. (1968), *The Nursery Years*, Routledge and Kegan Paul, London.

Katz, L. (1993), Lecture on 'Engaging Children's Minds' at the University of North London.

Katz, L. and Chard, S. (1989), *Engaging Children's Minds – the Project Approach*, Ablex Publishing Corporation.

Kerr, J. (1973), *The Tiger who came to tea*, Harpercollins, London.

Kress, G. (1995), *Making signs and making subjects: the English curriculum and social futures*, Inaugural Lecture, Institute of Education, London.

Laevers, F. (1993), 'Deep Level Learning', *European Early Childhood Research*, Vol 1, No 1, pp 53–68.

Laevers, F. (1994), 'The Innovative Project Experiential Education and the Definition of Quality in Education', *Studia Pedagogica*, 16, pp 159–72.

Laevers, F. (1995), Lecture at Worcester College.

Laevers, F. (1997), *A Process-Oriented Child Follow-up System for Young Children*, Centre for Experiential Education, Leuven.

Lee, V. and Das Gupta, P. (1995), *Children's Cognitive and Language Development*, OU Press, Milton Keynes.

Mairs, K., Stone, R. and Young, E. (1990), *Learning to be Strong: Developing assertiveness with young children*, Pen Green Centre, Changing Perspectives, Northwich.

Malcolm, A. (1993), *Father's Involvement with Their Children and Outside Work Commitments*, Unpublished study submitted as part of a Diploma in Post-Qualifying Studies.

Matthews, J. (1994), *Helping Children to Paint and Draw in Early Childhood*, Hodder and Stoughton, London.

McDougall in Nicholls, B. (1986), *Rumpus Schema Extra*, Cleveland Teachers in Education (LEA).

McLellan, E. (1997), 'The Importance of Counting' in Thompson, I. *Teaching and Learning Early Numbers*, Buckingham: Open University Press.

Meade, A. with Cubey, P. (1995), *Thinking Children*, New Zealand Council for Educational Research, Wellington.

Meek, M. (1982), *Learning to Read*, Bodley Head, London.

Miller, L. (1992), *Understanding Your 4 year old*, Rosendale Press, London.

Miller, P.H. (1989; 2nd Edition), *Theories of Developmental Psychology*, Freeman, New York.

Moll, L.C. (Ed) (1990, reprinted 1994), *Vygotsky and Education*, Cambridge University Press, Cambridge.

Moll, L.C. and Greenberg, J.B. (1990), Chapter entitled 'Creating zones of possibilities: Combining social contexts' in Moll, L.C. (Ed) (1990), *Vygotsky and Education*, Cambridge University Press, Cambridge.

Nash, J.M. (1997), 'Fertile minds' in *Time* Magazine, 3 February 1997.

Nicholls, R. (Ed) (1986), *Rumpus Schema Extra*, Cleveland Teachers in Education (LEA).

Nisbet, J. and Schucksmith, J. (1986), *Learning Strategies*, Routledge and Kegan Paul, London.

Nunes, T., Schliemann, A.D. and Carraher, D.W. (1993), *Street mathematics and school mathematics*, Cambridge University Press.

Nunes, T. (1995), Chapter entitled 'Mathematical and Scientific Thinking' in Lee, V. and Das Gupta, P. (Eds) (1995), *Children's Cognitive and Language Development*, OU Press, Milton Keynes.

Nunes, T. (1998), *Developing children's minds through literacy and numeracy*, Inaugural Lecture, Institute of Education, London.

Nutbrown, C. (1994), *Threads of Thinking*, Paul Chapman, London.

Oates, J. (Ed) (1994), *The Foundation of Child Development*, Blackwell, Oxford.

Oram, H. (1993), *Angry Arthur*, Red Fox, London.

Pascal, C. and Bertram, A.D. (1997), *Effective Early Learning*, Hodder and Stoughton, London.

Piaget, J. (1926, 1959), *The Language and Thought of the Child*, Routledge and Kegan Paul Ltd., London.

Piaget, J. (1936 – translation 1953), *The Origin of Intelligence in the Child*, Routledge and Kegan Paul, Ltd., London.

Piaget, J. (1937 – translation 1955), *The Child's Construction of Reality*, Routledge and Kegan Paul, Ltd., London.

Piaget, J. (1951, 1972), *Play, Dreams and Imitation in Childhood*, William Heinemann Ltd., London.

Piaget, J., Grize, J.B., Szeminska, A. and Vinh-Bang (1968), 'Epistemologie et Psychologie de la Fonction', *Etudes D'Epistemologie Genetique*, xxiii, Press Universitaires de France, cited in Athey, C. (1990), *Extending Thought in Young Children*, Paul Chapman, London.

Pinker, S. (1994), *The Language Instinct*, Penguin, London.

Pollard, A. (1996), *The Social World of Children's Learning*, Cassell, London.

Pope, A. (1985), *Pope*, Penguin, London

Read, C. (1975), 'Children's Categorization of Speech Sounds in English'. Urbana, I.L.: National Council of Teachers in English.

Rice, S. (1996), *An Investigation of Schemas as a Way of Supporting and Extending*

Young Children's Learning, unpublished dissertation as part of M.Ed, University of West of England.

Richardson, K. (1995), Chapter entitled 'The Development of Intelligence' in Lee, V. and Das Gupta, P. (1995), *Children's Cognitive and Language Development*, OU Press, Milton Keynes.

Riley, J. (1995), 'The Transition Phase between Emergent Literacy and Conventional Beginning Reading: New Research Findings', *Early Years*, Vol 16 No 1.

Roberts, R. (1995), *Self-Esteem and Successful Early Learning*, Hodder and Stoughton, London.

Rueda, R. (1990), Chapter entitled 'Assisted Performance in Writing' in Moll, L.C. (Ed)(1990), *Vygotsky and Education*, Cambridge University Press, Cambridge.

Rutter, M. and Rutter, M. (1992), *Developing Minds*, Penguin Group, London.

Schaffer, H.R. and Emerson, P.E. (1964b), 'Patterns of response to physical contact in early human development' *J. Child Psychol, Psychiat.*, **5,** 1–13.

Schaffer, H.R. (1998), 'Joint involvement episodes as context for cognitive development' in McGurk, H. (Ed) *Contemporary Issues in Childhood Social Development*, Routledge, London.

Schaffer, R. (1995), *Early Socialization*, British Psychological Society, Leicester.

Schaffer, H.R. (1996), Chapter entitled 'Joint Involvement Episodes' in Daniels. H. (Ed) (1996), *An Introduction to Vygotsky*, Routledge, London.

Schaffer, H.R. (1996), *Social Development*, Blackwell, Oxford.

Shaw, J. (1991), *An Investigation of Parents' Conceptual Development in the Context of Dialogue with a Community Teacher*, Ph.D Thesis, Newcastle University.

Stern, D. (1985), *The Interpersonal World of the Infant*, Basic Books Inc, U.S.

Tizard, B. and Hughes, M. (1984), *Young Children Learning*, Fontana, London.

Tizard, B. (1986), *The Care of Young Children*. Implications of Recent Research, University of London Institute of Education, London.

Tulloch, S. (1990), *Complete Wordfinder*. Oxford: Oxford University Press.

Van der Veer, R. and Valsiner, J. (1994), *The Vygotsky Reader*, Blackwell, Oxford.

Vygotsky, L.S. (1962), *Thoughts and Language*, M.I.T. Press and Wiley and Sons, London.

Webb, L. (1975), *Making a Start on Child Study*, Basil Blackwell, Oxford.

Weinberger, J. (1996), *Literacy goes to School – the parents' role in young children's literacy learning*, Paul Chapman, London.

Whalley, M. (1994), *Learning to be Strong – Setting up a neighbourhood service for under-fives and their families*, Hodder and Stoughton, London.

Whalley, M. (Ed) (1997), *Working with Parents*, Hodder and Stoughton, London.

White in J.M. and M.J. Cohen (1993), *The New Penguin Dictionary of Quotations*, London: Penguin.

Whitehead, M. (1997), *Language and Literacy in the Early Years*, Second Edition, Paul Chapman, London.

Winnicott, D.W. (1975), *Through Pediatrics to Psychoanalysis*, Hogarth Press, London.

Woodhead, M. et al (1995), 'Developmental perspectives on emotion' in Barnes, P. (Ed), *Personal, Social and Emotional Development of Children*, Open University Press, Milton Keynes.

INDEX

References to authors of research are not included in the index.